BURIED IN BOOKS

BURIED IN BOOKS

A Reader's Anthology

Julie Rugg

FRANCES LINCOLN LIMITED
PUBLISHERS

For Chris

BURIED IN BOOKS
Frances Lincoln Limited
4 Torriano Mews
Torriano Avenue
London NW5 2RZ
www.franceslincoln.com

Introduction copyright © Julie Rugg 2010
For full acknowledgments, see page 215
First Frances Lincoln edition: 2010

ISBN: 978-0-7112-2923-5

Printed and bound in China
by South China Printing Co. Ltd

2 4 6 8 9 7 5 3 1

CONTENTS

INTRODUCTION

Booklovers would like to appear sage and superior. In reality, the mania associated with acquiring, reading and simply messing about with books can be downright grubby. I have myself succumbed to the worst symptoms of this mania and have come through the other side a touch wiser but still – like a recovering addict – prone to spectacular lapses. Too often I wander out of a second-hand bookshop with a blush and a bag that is just a little too heavy. When I get home I hide the purchases by spreading them about on existing piles of books, so my husband won't notice. It's a method learned from the tunnellers in *The Great Escape*, and I heartily recommend it.

Hunting down fellow bibliomaniacs is an agreeable compulsion, and anthologizing their behaviour through the ages has become something of an addiction. Some people I have come to like tremendously. Hugh Walpole, for example, began modestly as an unstoppable reader but his passion for collecting accelerated exponentially as his income increased. At the end of his life he was said to have possessed 30,000 volumes. The sheer bulk of his collection overcame all attempts to order and catalogue: he simply waded about in books. If he couldn't place his hand on the title he wanted, he bought another copy and as a consequence his collection contained many duplicates. It was the same for William Gladstone, who bought and sold whole libraries at a time; book dealers were often able to sell his own books back to him, and he didn't notice. I wonder if this was better or worse than the mania of librarian Antonio Magliabechi, who died in 1714. He appeared to know exactly where in the world every book was at any given time. I can forgive Hugh and even Mr Gladstone, since both were monumental, marathon readers to whom respect is due. Magliabechi, on the other hand, is just a little bit spooky. The fact that he also liked spiders more than people is something of a giveaway.

Despite sharing in many of the manic elements of book love, I have to confess that I am a rubbish reader. I'm impatient and I skip. I try and pretend that this is because I'm discerning but often I can be just lazy. In the majority of the novels I read – especially ones written by Iris Murdoch – I forget who everyone is unless I make a plan and I tend not to make plans very often. *The Forsyte Saga* defeated me entirely, even though it provided a plan so I didn't have to make one. But now and again a writer throws my complacency and I have to listen and think very hard indeed: each sentence is just so very good it can't be bolted. I try and do those kinds of book maybe just three or four times a year, and I sneak back and reread on special occasions. It doesn't do to be spoiled.

Two things keep me reading and have me addicted for sure. First, I can't resist a good tale. I like stories where people lose everything in order to find out who they are; I like books that inadvertently, accidentally, educate me about something I didn't even know I knew nothing about; I like books that plunge into a foreign landscape and leave the reader to hack their way through; I love stories that have an 'oh my God!' twist or even two. I still remember that cracking big shock that's in *The Moonstone*. Even not very good books with a fine plot will have me – like Henry Crabb Robinson – speeding to the end just to see how it all plays out.

The second thing that keeps me reading is the absolute clarity that some writers achieve. It's the point that has me saying loud in my head, 'yes, that's like it is.' George Eliot is like that: her people are immediately real, and I'm not sure if any other author has been so perceptive. But many, many books will have at least one observation, one analogy, one single turn of phrase that makes the entire read worthwhile. So I will always plump for the tomes that I hope are orchards, with truths there to pluck from every page. However, junk is fine too and I'm happy with any detective who has a drink problem, Victorian melodrama or – when things are looking otherwise bleak – something that nearly won the Booker ten years ago, picked up in a library sale. Other people's taste in reading-to-pass-the-time is impossible to fathom, and it's best not to judge.

Of all the themes in this collection, I have most enjoyed the forays into the literature of bookselling and dealing. There are few great or even adequate novels where this is a central concern, and coming very highly recommended are: Laurence Block's series featuring the bookshop-owning burglar Bernie Rhodenbarr; Perez-Reverte's *Dumas Club*; Iain Sinclair's visceral but rather involved *White Chappell, Scarlet Tracings*, and – if you can get hold of a copy – Driff's *Guide to Bookdealers*. This is not a novel, but remains a remarkably good read. Driff was a grumpy old man long before grumpy was fashionable. Indeed, my first great book binge happened through the summer of '86 in London, when Driff was always in my pocket. This was the very best way to discover the mustier byways of the capital and further afield too.

Edinburgh also used to be a great place for a book trawl and may still be yet. I hear that West Port Books is under new ownership: its dark, looming shelves invariably contained something worth buying as did the shop round the corner from there, owned by a guy who – somewhat predictably – always wore a kilt. But there's still McNaughtan's down the stairs opposite the much lauded Valvona and Crolla at the top of Leith Walk, or there was last time I looked and I hope it thrives. There are fewer and fewer towns and cities that contain a string of truly excellent second-hand bookshops, where it's possible to swap a couple of notes for an armful of unexpected treasure. I've heard it said that you can shop for books on the Internet, but it sounds like a passionless exercise: a mere marriage of convenience. In reality, many readers do not know they want a book until they see it, touch it, smell it and fall a little in love with its promise. I know I'm not the only person who's bought a book just because of the way it sits in my hand.

This leads me to the contention that simply messing around with books is one of the very best ways to pass time that there is. Not necessarily reading, but just ambling about the house nonchalantly moving an armful of books from one place to another or creating a mountain of open volumes that's then abandoned because an entire other mountain in another room looks more interesting. Someone reordering their record collection by date or by alphabet or by genre will understand a similar compulsion in a house full of books. When books come into a house in a constant trickle there's always reshelving to be done and failures to weed out, borrowings to go back to their owners and the awful decision to be made about what to read next.

Another theme I like that's emerged from the most recent travels in the world of bookishness is tales about the mistreatment of books. For a booklover, these are like mini-horror stories that send a little frisson of fear down the spine. It is clear that Coleridge was a serial offender, but it's impossible not to smile at Lamb's despair on finding that yet another of his volumes had caught the poet's attention, knowing the book won't be returned in any fit state. Some people are unremitting in the protection they afford the books they own. The habit of buying from jumble sales means that I tend not to be too distracted by bumps and foxing and sunning and all the other charming words used by proper book people. However, having to use a university library means that I frequently handle books where the text has been high-lighted enthusiastically. Some students seem unaware that using a neon-coloured pen is not the same as reading. It always makes me cringe, and puts me in mind of graffiti on the Underground.

But this maltreatment is a reminder that each book has a life. Some are very short. A lot of contemporary political biographies go from printer to warehouse to shop to pulp factory before the ink is dry, and it's sad to see a book that will never, ever be loved or even welcomed. I can't recall off-hand a whole novel about a book's life, but it could be a worthy tale. I have in my possession just one valuable and extremely arcane antiquarian book, which dates from 1839. I hear rumours that Gladstone read the book – not this very one, as far as I know – and it would be nice to think that my copy travelled a little in elevated circles before coming to rest on my shelf. Suddenly I wonder where the book was during the war and whether it had any close calls or if it just sat in a library somewhere for a hundred years, subject only to the flick of a feather duster.

Library books probably have a more thrilling life than most. Jules Verne had the vision of a library where books would leave the shelves and then be handed on from reader to reader and only eventually return to the shelves, years later, and not a little dog-eared. I used to pencil my name in books as I bought them, and then erase the mark when I passed it on. Now I leave the mark, because I've come to like reading the names and inscriptions and notes left inside books as they move from owner to owner. I've even been tempted to buy a book because it has a remarkably styl-ish bookplate: who wouldn't want to be associated – albeit remotely – with someone who has impeccable taste? Even post-war municipal library markings can have a utilitarian allure.

I feel mute with shame at the realization that the last anthology made rather more jokes at the expense of librarians than really should have been the case. This collection aims to underline my true belief that librarianship is a noble calling. All the knowledge of the world is made freely accessible by libraries, to anyone with the wit to wander into them; it's librarians who smooth the pathway. I can't pretend to be even nearly as useful. The closest I have been to the job of librarian is as a volunteer who delivered books to remarkably genteel housebound ladies in Stirling. As might be expected, they were consumed by an appetite for violent crime novels although one customer had an inexplicable liking for Miss Read. The ladies pushed aside the tasking, involved and essentially wearying selection of South American novels I literally pedalled from door to door and brightened up when a new James Lee Burke fell out of the basket.

With a small coterie of exceptions, women are noticeably absent from literary accounts of bibliomania. Amongst the quotations here, women are usually only present to be impressed by bookishness and on no account can be allowed to display any of the nerdier bibliophilic symptoms. Perhaps this is because men can continue to indulge manic behaviours long into adult life, but women invariably have to grow up. It was something of a relief when my own particularly virulent strain of the book disease was cured by having a family. Prams have no place in second-hand bookshops – literally, there's usually no room to get one in – and tend to get in the way when barging forward into the bunfight of a Feed the Minds or Christian Aid book sale. Prams can be useful as a means of book transport, but then it is tiresome deciding where to leave the baby. Having a family also meant I had to stop the remarkably complex and fastidious method I had pursued – since a teenager – of recording and cataloguing my purchases. Some kind of barrier was shattered when my baby was born. I called up Oxfam: they carted away sacks full of books, and *I didn't even write down what I'd given them!* This put an unforgivable hole in my scrupulously maintained data relating to my own bookish behaviour, and I still don't feel quite right about it.

All of which brings us back to the fact that book love so often evokes the most egregious vices. An acquaintance of mine who is otherwise generous with their time and even money is downright mean when it comes to books. They laud a book to the degree that wanting to read it becomes a physical ache, waft their hand towards it sitting invitingly on their shelf, but on no account does the book ever leave their possession. One careful owner. Other people I know are very clear about the impression they want books to give of their intellectual capacities. In all the academic offices I've been in, I've never found a copy of Foucault that shows any sign of having been read; Baudrillard looks similarly pristine. And I must confess that I have myself stolen a book. It was *Three Men in a Boat* and I took it from a library cupboard while I was in the school dinner queue. I was snorting within the first few lines, and simply couldn't put it back. I still have the book, and reread it every couple of years. I could argue that I rescued rather than stole it, since the last stamp had been some time in the fifties: the book had been criminally underappreciated.

The collection ends in shadow. Faint-hearted book lovers might well conclude at chapter thirteen, and continue no further. The thought of having nothing to read is a terror too great to be borne. Almost all the situations where I have found myself with nothing to read have involved long-delayed trains, usually very late at night. Things have sometimes worked out OK. On one occasion my only book was *Trainspotting*. I finished it with many miles to go, and no other book in my bag. I mentally shrugged and turned back to page one and started again. It was actually better the second time, and had GNER not failed I would never have found that out. On a three-week trek around Mexico I took a selection of junk and books I wanted to be seen reading. I had bolted all the junk by the time I got to the departure lounge. This left me with *The Making of the English Working Class*. I couldn't get much beyond it being about Methodism and, until I found another traveller willing to swap their junk books for mine, I was compelled to read and reread my guide book. It was not a holiday I would care to repeat.

This introduction finishes with two housekeeping notes. First, all the quotations here are fully referenced, and the copyright notices indicate just how troublesome is the task of securing permissions. Thanks and even more thanks are due to the living authors who have so graciously given up quotations with little more than a murmur of good wishes. The big corporate estate-holders are scary monsters operated by surprisingly nice people, and so thanks too for their sleek efficiency. There's an index of authors, to help in the search for favourites. There is a subject index too, since a well-indexed book is both a friend and a resource; however, I would make no claims for it being even remotely reliable.

Second, acknowledgments can be a complex business. Here I simply thank Lynda Murphy, and not just for reading Hardy so I didn't have to.

I. 'A CHARMING ECCENTRICITY'

Degrees of bibliomania

The love of books is a charming eccentricity: it is respectable, it is innocent, it proves that you have an honest soul, a
contented mind.

> Jules Janin, quoted by E.V. Lucas in 'The *guide* supreme' (1936).

It is always more pleasant to meet with one who is a
bookman than with one who is not. I always feel safe and
comfortable and happy in the presence of any one who is
really fond of reading.

> W. Robertson Nicoll, *A Bookman's Letters* (1913).

I'm a reader for lots of reasons. On the whole, I tend to
hang out with readers, and I'm scared they wouldn't want to
hang out with me if I stopped.

> Nick Hornby, *The Complete Polysyllabic Spree* (2006).

It's not that I don't like people. It's just that when I'm in
the company of others – even my nearest and dearest – there
always comes a moment when I'd rather be reading a book.

> Maureen Corrigan, *Leave Me Alone: I'm Reading* (2005).

*****

I saw a girl sitting on a stone bench near. She was bent
over a book, on the perusal of which she seemed intent. From
where I stood I could see the title – it was *Rasselas* – a name
that struck me as strange, and consequently attractive. In

turning a leaf she happened to look up, and I said to her directly –

'Is your book interesting?' I had already formed the intention of asking her to lend it to me some day.

'I like it,' she answered, after a pause of a second or two, during which she examined me.

'What is it about?' I continued. I hardly know where I found the hardihood thus to open a conversation with a stranger. The step was contrary to my nature and habits; but I think her occupation touched a chord of sympathy somewhere, for I, too, liked reading, though of a frivolous and childish kind. I could not digest or comprehend the serious or substantial.

'You may look at it,' replied the girl, offering me the book.

I did so. A brief examination convinced me that the contents were less taking than the title. *Rasselas* looked dull to my trifling taste. I saw nothing about fairies, nothing about genii; no bright variety spread over the closely-printed pages. I returned it to her.

Charlotte Bronte, *Jane Eyre* (1847).

Travelled home in an infernally hot train crowded with soldiers, sailors and ATS: the only available seat was in the corridor on a suitcase opposite the lavatory, from which a stench of urine poured, and edged in by hot soldiers in their thick uniforms, mopping their foreheads and complaining of thirst. One carried a pile of poetry books.

Frances Partridge, diary entry 20th June 1941.

DICKIE (*starting to write on the back of a postcard*) I love the fact you brought Shakespeare with you and no clothes. Ermelinda says you wash the same shirt out every night. Is that true?

Anthony Minghella, *The Talented Mr Ripley: A Screenplay* (2000).

LUCY Indeed, ma'am, I traversed half the town in search of it: I don't believe there's a circulating library in Bath I ha'n't been at.

LYDIA And could you not get *The Reward of Constancy*?

LUCY No, indeed, ma'am.

LYDIA Not *The Fatal Connection*?

LUCY No, indeed, ma'am.

LYDIA Nor *The Mistakes of the Heart*?

LUCY Ma'am, as ill-luck would have it, Mr Bull said Miss Sukey Saunter had just fetched it away.

LYDIA Heigh-ho! – did you inquire for *The Delicate Distress*?

LUCY Or *Memoirs of Lady Woodford*? Yes indeed, ma'am. I asked everywhere for it and I might have brought it from Mr Frederick's but Lady Slattern Lounger, who had just sent it home, had so soiled and dog's eared it, it wa'n't fit for a Christian to read.

LYDIA Heigh-ho! – yes I always know when Lady Slattern has been before me. She has a most observing thumb; and I believe cherishes her nails for the convenience of making marginal notes. Well, child, what *have* you brought me?

LUCY Oh! here ma'am. [*taking books from under her cloak, and from her pockets*] This is *The Gordian Knot* – and this *Peregrine Pickle*. Here are *The Tears of Sensibility*, and *Humphrey Clinker*. This is *The Memoirs of a Lady of Quality*, written by herself – and here the second volume of *The Sentimental Journey*.

LYDIA Heigh-ho! – what are those books by the glass?

LUCY The great one is only *The Whole Duty of Man* – where I press a few blondes, ma'am.

LYDIA Very well – give me the *sal volatile*.

LUCY Is it in a blue cover, ma'am?

Richard Brinsley Sheridan, *The Rivals* (c.1773).

Books are becoming everything to me. If I had at this moment my choice of life, I would bury myself in one of those immense libraries that we saw together at the universities, and never pass a waking hour without a book before me.

Thomas Babington Macaulay, letter to Margaret Cropper, 1834.

How happy was Emily at that moment! She could scarcely contain herself until the book was fetched, and when it arrived she buried herself so earnestly in its pages as to win smiles of sympathy and approval from the blasé veterans of the Reading Room, to whom, for more years than they cared to count, the first glance at the book they had ordered had begot nothing but a dyspeptic desire for yet another.

John Collier, *His Monkey Wife* (1930).

At the moment of freedom from school I plunged down side streets to the library, left the three volumes that I had borrowed a day of two before, climbed a wabbling ladder to the dark mysteries beneath the ceiling, and had a glorious dirty half hour of choosing and rejecting . . . shaking dust from the bodies of Bage and Ferrier, Godwin and Henry Mackenzie, Eugène Sue (I read the whole of 'The Wandering Jew' in a week) and G.P.R. James. I had no guide to any of these things; I had at this time read no books of literary criticism, I had no notion of anyone's dates or characteristics or personal histories, I simply nuzzled and nuzzled and chewed and chewed. I have said that the danger of this proceeding was that I never stopped to think. I found 'Frankenstein' and 'A Fool of Quality' and 'The Romance of the Forest' (heaven's blessing on Mrs Radcliffe) and 'Sidney Biddulph' all equally good and splendid. The dust hovered in clouds about my devoted head, the ladder quivered and quivered again as though with sympathetic agitation at my ecstasies, the Canons and the Canon's wives came in, fought their battles over the newer books and retreated, the afternoon passed and the night wore on, and just before closing time I would be seen emerging surreptitiously as though I had committed some crime, my face grimed, my school cap awry, and *Destiny* in three stout volumes under my arm.

Hugh Walpole, *These Diversions: Reading* (1926).

I remember that, when I was fourteen, we lived about two miles from the nearest library. I had a choice. I could cycle there, borrow my books, and cycle back in a very few minutes – but those few minutes were lost to reading. Or, if I wished, I could walk to the library, reading the last fifty or seventy-five pages of my calculatedly unfinished book en route, make my borrowings, and walk back, reading a new volume on the way. I usually preferred the latter procedure. It is no trick at all to read while walking, to step off and on to kerbs with unconscious skill, to avoid other pedestrians while your eyes are riveted to the page. There was a special pleasure in it: I had outwitted Father Time.

Clifton Fadiman, *Reading I've Liked* (1946).

He'd read far too many books, that was Israel's trouble.

Books had spoilt him; they had curdled his brain, like cream left out on a summer afternoon, or eggs overbeaten with butter. He'd been a bookish child, right from the off, the youngest of four, the kind of child who seemed to start reading without anyone realising or noticing, who enjoyed books without his parents' insistence, who raced through non-fiction at an early age and an extraordinary rate, who read Jack Kerouac before he was in his teens, and who by the age of sixteen had covered most of the great French and Russian authors, and who as a result had matured into an intelligent, shy, passionate, sensitive soul, full of dreams and ideas, a wide-ranging vocabulary, and just about no earthly good to anyone.

Ian Sansom, *The Mobile Library: The Case of the Missing Books* (2005).

Mrs Cayhill was a handsome woman, who led a comfortable, vegetable existence, and found it a task to rise from the plump sofa-cushion. Her pleasant features were slack, and in those moments of life which called for a sudden decision, they wore the helpless bewilderment of a woman who has never been required to think for herself. Her grasp on practical matters was rendered the more lax, too, by her being an immoderate reader, who fed on novels from morning till night, and slept with a page turned down beside her bed. She was forever lost in the joys or sorrows of some fictitious person, and, in consequence, remained for the most part completely ignorant of what was going on around her. When she did happen to become conscious of her surroundings, she was callous, or merely indifferent, to them; for, compared with romance, life was dull and diffuse; it lacked the wilful simplicity; the exaggerated omissions, and forcible perspectives, which make up art; in other words, life demanded that unceasing work of selection and rejection, which it is the story-teller's duty to perform for his readers. All novels were fish to Mrs Cayhill's net; she lived in a world of intrigue and excitement and, seated in her easy-chair by the sitting-room window, was generally as remote from her family as though she were in Timbuctoo.

Henry Handel Richardson, *Maurice Guest* (1908).

Of course it can be carried to an excess; and a man may become a mere book-eater, as a man may become an opium-eater. I used at one time to go and stay with an old friend, a clergyman in a remote part of England. He was a bachelor and fairly well off. He did not care about exercise or his garden, and he had no taste for general society. He subscribed to the London Library and to a lending library in the little town where he lived, and he bought, too, a good many books. He must have spent, I used to calculate, about ten hours of the twenty-four in reading. He seemed to me to have read everything, old and new books alike, and he had an astonishing memory; anything that he put into his mind remained there exactly as fresh and clear as when he laid it away, so that he never needed to read a book twice. If he had lived at a University he would have been a useful man; if one wanted to know what books to read in any line, one had only to pick his brains. He could give one a list of authorities on almost every subject. But in his country parish he was entirely thrown away. He had not the least desire to make anything of his stores, or to write. He had not the art of expression, and he was a distinctly tiresome talker. His idea of a conservation was to ask you whether you had read a number of modern novels. If he found one that you had not read, he sketched the plot in an intolerably prolix manner, so that it was practically impossible to fix the mind on what he was saying. He seemed to have no preferences in literature whatever; his one desire was to read everything that came out, and his only idea of a holiday was to go up to London and get lists of books from a bookseller. That is, of course, an extreme case; and I cannot help feeling that he would have been nearly as usefully employed if he had confined himself to counting the number of words in the books he read.

A.C. Benson, 'Books' (1906).

I have known men and women who read so voraciously and continuously that they never have the time or opportunity to discover who they really are. Indeed, I suspect it is precisely because they prefer not to make that discovery that they cling limpet-like to books. I suppose this is better for them than alcohol or hasheesh but it is not very different. All of us, I am sure, have noticed people who suffer from reader's fidgets. If there is a book, a magazine, any piece of print within easy reach, they will at once take it up, idly, without real intent to peruse it, but out of a mechanical compulsion. They will do this while they are talking to you, while you are talking to them, while engaged in some other activity. They are the victims of print.

Clifton Fadiman, *Reading I've Liked* (1946).

Now he would prowl the stacks of the library at night, pulling books out of a thousand shelves and reading in them like a madman. The thought of these vast stacks of books would drive him mad; the more he read, the less he seemed to know – the greater the number of books he read, the greater the immense uncountable number of those which he could never read would seem to be. Within a period of ten years he read at least 20,000 volumes – deliberately the number is set low – and opened the pages and looked through many times that number. This may seem unbelievable, but it happened. Dryden said this about Ben Jonson: 'Other men read books, but he reads libraries' – and so now it was with this boy. Yet this terrific orgy of the books brought him no comfort, peace, or wisdom of the mind and heart. Instead, his fury and despair increased from what they fed upon, his hunger mounted with the food it ate.

He read insanely, by the hundreds, the thousands, the ten thousands, yet he had no desire to be bookish; no one could describe this mad assault upon print as scholarly: a ravening appetite to him demanded that he read everything that had ever been written about human experience. He read no more from pleasure – the thought that other books were waiting for him tore at his heart for ever. He pictured himself as tearing the entrails from a book as from a fowl. At first, hovering over book-stalls, or walking at night among the vast piled shelves of the library, he would read, watch in hand, muttering to himself in triumph or anger at the timing of each page: 'Fifty seconds to do that one. Damn you, we'll see! You will, will you?' – and he would tear through the next page in twenty seconds.

Thomas Wolfe, *Of Time and the River* (1935).

In short, he so buried himself in his books that he spent the nights reading from twilight till daybreak and the days from dawn till dark; and so from little sleep and much reading, his brain dried up and he lost his wits.

Miguel Cervantes, *Don Quixote* (1614).

*****

Book lovers always have to touch books.

Maureen Corrigan, *Leave Me Alone: I'm Reading* (2005).

Mr Dobson, for example, writes charmingly of his favourites on the unglazed shelves: the bulged and the bruised octavos, the dear and the dumpy twelves; and Mr Dobson's disciples who pursue the same convention are many, both here and in America, where indeed book-loving in public is carried to a point that is has never reached in England, the possessors of treasured tomes caressing them in the broad light of day as if there were no such thing as shame at all.

E.V. Lucas, 'Other people's books' (1909).

*****

A large share of my allowance was appropriated to my literary wants. I cannot forget the joy with which I exchanged a bank-note of twenty pounds for the twenty volumes of the *Memoirs of the Academy of Inscriptions*; nor would it have been easy, by any other expenditure of the same sum, to have procured so large and lasting a fund of rational amusement.

Edward Gibbon, *The Autobiography of Edward Gibbon* (1796).

But his chief hobby was to collect books, a weakness of which he was most heartily ashamed . . . There are stories of Uncle Charles as a young man slinking upstairs with armfuls of books, which he hid under the bed. They were still there when he died, hundreds of them. In fact the bed actually rested on books. The walls of his room were covered with them. The rest were stored in an enormous damp and dingy cellar beneath some shops in Gray's Inn Road, and tended by a bricklayer of grubby appearance and uncertain habits. It was the bricklayer's business to spend his evenings opening the various packages which had been thrown down the stairs by delivery boys during the day, and to arrange them on the shelves, and as Uncle Charles appeared to be the mainstay and support of most of the second-hand booksellers in London, the bricklayer could not keep pace with the deliveries, and the accumulation of unopened packets was at times enormous. It was very rarely that anyone else was allowed to enter that cellar. I do not think the owner spent much time there. If a particular book was asked for he promised readily to get it, but more often than not it was never found.

Malcolm Letts, *The Old House* (1942).

And Boulard! Boulard, the greatest buyer of old books this century has seen; Boulard, the old notary whose face and memory are unforgettable. He was the most thorough-going of bibliomaniacs. He bought books by the metre, by the toise, by the acre! He bought in detail, in block, by the basket, by the heap; his drawing-room, his vestibules, his lumber-rooms, his stairs, his bedrooms, his cupboards bent under the weight of his volumes.

Octave Uzanne, *The Book-Hunter in Paris* (1893).

His habits of life were uniform. Ever among his books, he troubled himself with no other concern whatever; and the only interest he appeared to take for any living thing was his spiders; for whom, while sitting among his literary piles, he affected great sympathy . . . Heyman, a celebrated Dutch professor, visited this erudite librarian, who was considered as the ornament of Florence. He found him amongst his books, of which the number was prodigious. Two or three rooms in the first storey were crowded with them, not only along their sides, but piled in heaps on the floor, so that it was difficult to sit, and more so to walk. A narrow space was contrived, indeed, so that by walking sideways you might extricate yourself from one room to another. This was not all; the passage below stairs was full of books, and the staircase from the top to the bottom was lined with them. When you reached the second storey, you saw with astonishment three rooms, similar to those below, equally full, so crowded, that two good beds in these chambers were also crammed with books.

This apparent confusion did not, however, hinder Magliabechi from immediately finding the books he wanted. He knew them all so well, that even to the least of them it was sufficient to see its outside, to say what it was; and indeed he read them day and night, and never lost sight of any. He ate on his books, he slept on his books, and he quitted them as rarely as possible.

Isaac Disraeli, 'Magliabechi' (1807).

It was known that Klamm lived, slept and ate, if he did eat, in a council flat in Lambeth. Nobody had visited him in it, but booksellers' catalogues were sent to that address. It was rumoured in the trade, in the way that rumours become facts, that Klamm was a man of property, with holdings in India, with interests in Whitechapel. It was rumoured, it was whispered by young men in pinstripe suits and splashy ties, the Salon of the

Rejected, who spent their days gossiping at their desks, licking their lip gloss, part of the furniture of what pretended to be the leading establishment for the sale of Modern First Editions, meaning anything that looked good in a glass cabinet, it was whispered, it was mooted, the legend became fact, that Klamm owned a house somewhere, nowhere, Clerkenwell or Finsbury or Holborn, a house that was never opened to daylight, whose few articles of use had been left undisturbed, sheeted, whose rooms were filled with shelves, whose shelves were filled with books, each book wrapped in tissue paper, sealed, placed within a brown paper bag, sealed again: that there were rooms and rooms, shelf upon shelf, nothing but wrapped books, like looking into a burial ground, erased inscriptions, neat lines, the gravestones covered in stocking-masks.

Iain Sinclair, *White Chappell, Scarlet Tracings* (1987).

* * * * *

Books have many pleasing qualities for those who know how to choose them. But nothing good is without its evil side; this pleasure is no purer or more unmixed than any other. It has its disadvantages, and very grave ones. Books exercise the mind, but the body, whose interests I have never neglected either, remains inactive, and grows heavy and dull. I know of no excess that does me more harm, or that I should avoid more strictly in these my declining years.

Montaigne, 'On three kinds of relationships' (1580).

Indiscriminate love of books is a disease, like satyriasis, and stern measure should be applied to it.

Clifton Fadiman, *Reading I've Liked* (1946).

There is a great deal of humbug about bibliophiles.

Andrew Lang (1902).

2. 'RAPT CLEAN OF OURSELVES'

Reading

In anything fit to be called by the name of reading, the process itself should be absorbing and voluptuous; we should gloat over a book, be rapt clean of ourselves, and rise from the perusal, our mind filled with the busiest, kaleidoscopic dance of images, incapable of sleep or of continuous thought.

Robert Louis Stevenson, 'A gossip on romance' (1882).

I changed the topic, in despair, to the novels that were scattered about her.

'Can you find nothing there,' I asked, 'to amuse you this wet morning?'

'There are two or three good novels,' she said carelessly, 'but I read them before I left London.'

'And the others won't even do for a dull day in the country?' I went on.

'They might do for some people,' she answered, 'but not for me. I'm rather peculiar, perhaps, in my tastes. I'm sick to death of novels with an earnest purpose. I'm sick to death of outbursts of eloquence, and large-minded philanthropy, and graphic descriptions, and unsparing anatomy of the human heart, and all that sort of thing. Good gracious me! isn't the original intention or purpose, or whatever you call it, of a work of fiction to set out distinctly by telling a story? And how many of these books, I should like to know, do that? Why, so far as telling a story is concerned, the greater part of them might as well be sermons as novels. Oh, dear me! what I want is something that seizes hold of my interest, and makes me forget when it's time to dress for dinner; something that keeps me reading, reading, reading, in a breathless state to find out the end.

Wilkie Collins, *The Queen of Hearts* (1859).

On Thursday mornings, then, towards ten o'clock, I would often find my long-haired sister still abed and reading. Always pale and absorbed, she read in a grim kind of way, with a cup of chocolate grown cold beside her. She took no more heed of my arrival than of the cries of 'Get up, Juliette!' coming from below stairs. She would read on, mechanically twining one of her snake-like plaits round her wrist and sometimes turning towards me an unseeing glance, that sexless, ageless glance of the obsessed, full of obscure defiance and incomprehensible irony.

Colette, *My Mother's House* (1922).

*****

I have been reading the Chronicle of the Good Knight Messire Jacques de Lalain, curious but dull from the constant repetition of the same species of combats in the same style and phrase. It is like washing bushels of sand for a grain of gold. It passes the time however, especially in that listless mood when your mind is half on your book half on some thing else: you catch something to arrest the attention every now and then and what you miss is not worth going back upon.

Walter Scott, diary entry 19th February 1826.

That was when I got into the habit of binge-reading. It's easy to do when you spend hours of every day surrounded by more books than you can ever read. You start one but you're distracted by the idea that you could, equally, have started a different one. By the end of the day you've skimmed two and started four and read the ends of about seven. You can read your way through a library like that without ever properly finishing any of the books.

Scarlett Thomas, *The End of Mr Y* (2006).

We are never allowed to forget that some books are badly written; we should remember that sometimes they're badly read, too.

Nick Hornby, *The Complete Polysyllabic Spree* (2006).

We are in danger of automatic reading, a mechanical process which leaves scarcely more definite impression on the memory than does the winding of one's watch, or the bolting of the front door at night. Without boiling water we can't make tea. Attention is the boiling water of the mind, and without it there arises no fragrance or refreshment from our reading.

Edward Butler, 'A table talk on books and reading' (1885).

And yet, though I have read so much, I am a bad reader. I read slowly and I am a poor skipper. I find it difficult to leave a book, however bad and however much it bores me, unfinished. I could count on my fingers the number of books that I have not read from cover to cover. On the other hand there are few books that I have read twice. I know very well that there are many of which I cannot get the full value on a single reading, but in that they have given me all I was capable of getting at the time, and this, though I may forget their details, remains a permanent enrichment.

W. Somerset Maugham, *The Summing Up* (1938).

Now, I do not believe dogmatically either in fast or slow reading. I believe tripe should be read practically with the speed of light and, let us say, Toynbee's *A Study of History* with tortoise deliberation. And most books are nearer to tripe than to Toynbee. But the trouble with practically all of us is that we suffer from chronic reverence. We make the unwarranted assumption that because a man is in print he has something to say. This may be good manners, but it's a confounded waste of time.

Clifton Fadiman, *Reading I've Liked* (1946).

I think it is much better for a book to have some parts that can be skipped just as well as not, you get through it so much faster. I have often thought what a good thing it would be if somebody would write a book that we could skip the whole of. I think a good many people would like to have such a book as that. I know I should.

William Henry Frost, *Fairies and Folk of Ireland* (1900).

*****

For as to the devotees of the circulating libraries, I dare not compliment their pass-time, or rather kill-time, with the name of reading. Call it rather a sort of beggarly day-dreaming during which the mind of the dreamer furnishes for itself nothing but laziness and a little mawkish sensibility . . . We should therefore transfer this species of amusement . . . from the genus, reading, to that comprehensive class characterized by the power of reconciling the two contrary yet co-existing propensities of human nature, namely indulgence of sloth and hatred of vacancy. In addition to novels and tales of chivalry in prose or rhyme, (by which last I mean neither rhythm nor metre) this genus comprises as its species, gaming, swinging, or swaying on a chair or gate; spitting over a bridge; smoking; snuff-taking; tête-à-tête quarrels after dinner between husband and wife; conning word by word all the advertisements of the *Daily Advertizer* in a public house on a rainy day, etc. etc. etc.

Samuel Taylor Coleridge, *Biographia Literaria* (1817).

Gadding, gazing, lounging, mere pleasure-mongering, reading for the relief of ennui, – these are as useless as sleeping, or dozing, or the stupidity of a surfeit.

Henry Ward Beecher, 'Industry and idleness' (1882).

If a person given to reading were honestly to keep a register of all the printed stuff that he or she consumes in a year – all the idle tales of which the very names and the story are forgotten in a week, the bookmaker's prattle about nothing at so much a sheet, the fugitive trifling about silly things and empty people, the memoirs of the unmemorable, and lives of those who never really lived at all – of what a mountain of rubbish would it be the catalogue.

Frederic Harrison, *The Choice of Books
and Other Literary Pieces* (1896).

Home with a bad influenza cold. In a deplorable condition. The best I could do was sit by the fire and read newspapers one by one from the first page to the last till the reading became mechanical. I found myself reading an account of the Lincoln Handicap and a column article on Kleptomania, while the advertisements of new books were devoured with relish as delicacies. My mind became a morass of current Divorce Court News, Society Gossip – 'if Sir A. Goes Romeward, if Miss B. sings true' – and advertisements. I went on reading because I was afraid to be alone with myself.

W.N.P. Barbellion, diary entry 26th March 1914.

*****

There are certain delusions which prevail extensively and obstinately. One of them we all share. We all think we have a sense of humour. But when we go outside to the larger world and remember the people we meet there, we are well assured that many of them have no very keen sense of humour, and that some at least have no sense of humour at all. Another mighty delusion is that every one is fond of reading. Almost every one thinks he is. I never heard any one say, 'I do not care for reading; it bores me and worries me.' But I have heard very many say that they regret extremely that they have never been able to read as much as they would like. They never have had sufficient time. As a matter of fact, no one who really cared for reading was ever deterred from it by want of time.

W. Robertson Nicoll, *A Bookman's Letters* (1913).

I started reading again – I always was reading, or at least quite a few pages seemed to have gone by. I must admit, I admire the way in which Orwell starts his book fairly late in, on page seven. This has to work in your favour. Reading takes a long time, though, don't you find? It takes such a long time to get from, say, page twenty-one to page thirty. I mean, first you've got page twenty-three, then page twenty-five, then page twenty-*seven*, then page twenty-*nine*, not to mention the even numbers. Then page thirty. Then you've got page thirty-*one* and page thirty-*three* – there's no end to it. Luckily *Animal Farm* isn't that long a novel. But novels . . . they're all long, aren't they? I mean, they're all so *long*.

Martin Amis, *Money* (1984).

He had no knowledge of Montaigne, no more than is obtained from dozing off three nights in a row with a musty volume cradled in your lap. He had not even reached the second chapter (the one on idleness) before his pointed chin was digging into his chest and his reading glasses had fallen into his lap.

Peter Carey, *Oscar and Lucinda* (1988).

We fought, Wilkie Collins and I. We fought bitterly and with all our might, to a standstill, over a period of about three weeks, on trains and aeroplanes and by hotel swimming pools. Sometimes – late at night, in bed – he could put me out cold with a single paragraph; every time I got through twenty or thirty pages, it felt to me as though I'd socked him good, but it took a lot out of me, and I had to retire to my corner to wipe the blood and sweat off my reading glasses. And still he kept coming back for more. Only in the last fifty-odd pages, after I'd landed several of those blows, did old Wilkie show any signs of buckling under the assault. He was pretty tough for a man of one hundred and eighty. Hats off to him.

Nick Hornby, *The Complete Polysyllabic Spree* (2006).

*****

It is odd, is it not, that a chance glance at a magazine should alter a man's future. For years I have been consumed by an ambition to make a lasting contribution to English Letters, but apart from my popular index to the Rev. T.R. Pipe's *Flora and Fauna of Megthorpe and District* I have achieved little or nothing on which to base my claims to immortality. Now, however, I see my remaining years rich in promise. I dedicate them to the service of literature.

The magazine in question was American. I happened to read one of its short stories while waiting for an interview with my dentist. The story itself was unremarkable – a slight thing of amateur detection – but when I was about to turn the page my eye was arrested by an unusual sub-title: 'Reading Time – Eight Minutes.' Rather foolishly, I took this direction as a variation of such clichés as 'Time – the Present' and 'Ten Years Later' . . . and read through the story again thinking that I had omitted some subtle chronometrical point. After all, you never know with detective fiction writers.

I was so engrossed in the problem that I cancelled my appointment, borrowed the magazine and returned home. My atlas told me that there are several Readings in the United States. By allowing fifteen degrees longitude to one hour I worked out the deviations from Standard Time at each place, but I was still unable to account for the eight minutes. Now it is a marked trait in my character that, my interest once aroused, I will move heaven and earth to arrive at a satisfactory explanation. Accordingly I put the problem to my wife.

'You silly!' she said. 'It means that it takes eight minutes to read the story.'

I saw immediately what she meant and returned to my study to put the thesis to the test. It was correct. The novelty of the idea soon overcame my conservative distaste of commercialism in the arts and I realized that fate, acting in the interests of literature, had directed my unwilling steps to the dentist that day.

Already in my mind's eye I could see the title pages of the classics:

Vanity Fair (or something)
by W.M. Thackeray (or somebody)
Reading Time assessed by J. Sopwhittle
14 hrs 15 mins (or something).

If the plan already taking root in my brain should come to fruition the great treasures of literature would be revitalized. The English love of races and records might well be guided by a healthy competition into the serener pastures of learning. I had a new world in the making – a civilization where men were idolized not because they ran a hundred yards in May, because they made a thousand runs in ten seconds or because they made terrific breaks at gold, but because they read Dickens in 'evens,' Trollope in bus queues or *Ulysses* before breakfast.

There were other advantages too. The statisticians would be delighted and the libraries would be run on efficient lines. A borrower would not longer be expected to read *The Seven Pillars of Wisdom* and a novel by Beverley Nichols in the same length of time.

I began the monumental task immediately. Clearly the official Sopwhittle reading time must be average time – happy medium between that of the illiterate and that of the blasé reviewer. I invited the co-operation of my gardener and he began with *The Pilgrim's Progress*. When he died, four years later, I found from the discolouration of the pages that he had reached page 13. Other assistants have proved equally unsuitable. The scheme involved a considerable outlay of capital for the purchase of books – very few of which have so far been returned.

Six months ago I took stock of my position and decided to continue the work single-handed. There was only one disadvantage in the new decision – it meant that I should have to read the classics.

Bernard Hollowood, 'Reading time' (1948).

*****

I hope that reading aloud will continue to be encouraged in schools, against the revival of interest in it that the swing of the pendulum should ensure. My own schooldays in several establishments were sweetened by it, although the example of the master who was most addicted to this pleasant art may be held to have been a little dangerous. He was a handsome and (I now conjecture) profligate Scotchman, with a world record for some athletic feat – I think for throwing the hammer – and a tendency to be on sponging terms with the older boys and frankly piratical terms with the younger, for he still possesses (or at least I do not) a silver pencil of mine to which he took a fancy. What branch of learning he had under his control, I forget completely, but what I can remember, with minute fidelity, is the entertainment that he substituted for it; for it was his genial and popular habit to place beneath the text-book from which he should have instructed us – and indeed did affect to instruct us when any authority or a messenger from another class-room entered – either a play of Shakespeare or a novel of Ouida (his two authors) from which he read to us with fine feeling as long as the coast was clear. He was a born reader, his only fault being that he felt too much, and I can still see the tears streaming down his face over *A Leaf in the Storm* and *A Dog of Flanders* and other pathetic histories.

E.V. Lucas, 'On reading aloud' (1909).

The whole joy of reading aloud comes from the act of sharing; the known reactions of both parties in the undertaking; the mingling of emotions as the work slowly unfolds. For this reason the best books to read aloud are those neither party has read before. If there is acquaintance on the part of the listener then there is not much point in the work being read. In such circumstances attention will be concentrated on the delivery rather than the content, a course liable to lead to trouble. If the reader knows what is coming on the next page then he or she will be hard put to remain neutral. Expression will degenerate into histrionics.

Oliver Edwards, 'Reading aloud' (1957).

When the story was very interesting, Mrs Caldwell read until she was hoarse, and then went on to herself – 'dipping', the children called it. It was a point of honour with them not to dip, and they would remonstrate with their mother loudly when they caught her at it. Their feeling on the subject was so strong that she was ashamed to be seen dipping at last. She used to put the book away until they were safe in bed, and then gratify her curiosity; but they suspected her, because once or twice they noticed that she was unaffected by an exciting part; so one night they came down in their night-dresses and caught her, and after that the poor lady had to be careful. She might thump the children for coming downstairs, but she could not alter the low opinion they had of a person who dipped.

Sarah Grand, *The Beth Book* (1897).

Tommy became her favourite, and as he had taught himself to read, after a fashion, in London, where his lesson-books were chiefly placards and the journal subscribed to by Shovel's father, she often invited him after school hours to the blue-and-white room, where he sat on a kitchen chair (with his boots off) and read aloud, very slowly, while Miss Ailie knitted. The volume was from the Thrums Book Club, of which Miss Ailie was one of the twelve members. Each member contributed a book every year, and as their tastes in literature differed, all sorts of books came into the club, and there was one member who invariably gave a ro-ro-romance. He was double-chinned and forty, but the schoolmistress called him the dashing young banker, and for months she avoided his dangerous contribution. But always there came a black day when a desire to read the novel seized her, and she hurried home with it beneath her rokelay. This year the dashing banker's choice was a lady's novel called *I Love My Love with an A*, and it was a frivolous tale, those being before the days of the new fiction with its grand discovery that women have an equal right with men to grow beards. The hero had such a way with him and was so young (Miss Ailie could not stand them a day more than twenty) that the schoolmistress was enraptured and scared at every page, but she fondly hoped that Tommy did not understand. However, he discovered one day what something printed thus 'D—n' meant, and he immediately said the word with such unction that Miss Ailie let fall her knitting. She would have ended the readings then had not Agathy been at that point in the arms of an officer who, Miss Ailie felt for certain, had a wife in India, and so how could she rest till she knew for certain? To track the officer by herself was not to be thought of, to read without knitting being such a shameless waste of time, and it was decided to resume the readings on a revised plan: Tommy to say 'stroke' in place of the 'D—ns' and 'word we have no concern with' instead of 'Darling' and 'Little One'.

J.M. Barrie, *Sentimental Tommy* (1896).

I led up to it, saying to Eliza, not at all in a complaining way, 'Does it not seem to you a pity to let these long winter evenings run to waste?'

'Yes dear,' she replied, 'I think you ought to do something.'

'And you too. Is it not so, darling?'

'There's generally some sewing, or the accounts.'

'Yes; but these things do not exercise the mind.'

'Accounts do.'

'Not in the way I mean.' I had now reached my point. 'How would it be if I were to read aloud to you? I don't think you have ever heard me read aloud. You are fond of the theatre, and we cannot often afford to go. This would make up for it. There are many men who would tell you that they would sooner have a play read aloud to them than see it acted in the finest theatre in the world.'

'Would they? Well – perhaps – if I were only sewing it wouldn't interrupt me much.'

I said, 'That is not very graciously put, Eliza. There is a certain art in reading aloud. Some have it, and some have not. I do not know if I have ever told you, but when I was a boy of twelve I won a prize for recitation, though several older boys were competing against me.'

She said that I had told her several times.

I continued: 'And I suppose that I have developed since then. A man in our office once told me he thought I should have done well on the stage. I don't know whether I ever mentioned it.'

She said that I had mentioned it once or twice.

'I should have thought that you would have been glad of a little pleasure – innocent, profitable, and entertaining. However, if you think I am not capable of –'

'What would you want to read?'

'What would you like me to read?'

'Miss Sakers lent me this.' She handed me a paper-covered volume, entitled 'The Murglow Mystery; or, The Stain on the Staircase'.

'Trash like this is not literature,' I said. However, to please her, I glanced at the first page. Half an hour later I said that I should be very sorry to read a book of that stamp out loud.

'Then why do you keep reading it to yourself?'

'Strictly speaking, I am not reading it. I am glancing at it.'

When Eliza got up to go to bed, an hour afterwards, she asked me if I was still glancing.

'Try not to be so infernally unreasonable,' I said. 'If Miss Sakers lends us a book, it is discourteous not to look at it.'

Barry Pain, 'Shakespeare' (1900–13).

*****

I have lost my taste for reading, and there are few greater misfortunes. We cannot always be talking, we cannot always be at the theatre, we cannot always be listening to music or visiting exhibitions of pictures; and to lose one's taste for reading is really like losing one's taste for bread.

George Moore, *Conversations in Ebury Street* (1924).

3. 'SOMETIMES, PROFOUND EPIPHANIES'

The great virtue of literature is that by deepening our consciousness, by widening our perception of life, by giving shape to our feelings, it speaks to us as with a voice saying: All ideals and acts, all the world of the spirit is created out of the blood and nerves of men. It tells us that Hen-Toy, the Chinaman, is as agonizingly unsatisfied with the love of woman as Don Juan, the Spaniard; that the Abyssinian sings the same songs of sorrows and joys of love as the Frenchman; that there is an equal pathos in the love of a Japanese Geisha and Manon Lescaut; that man's longing to find in woman the other half of his soul has burned and burns with an equal flame men of all lands, all times.

A murderer in Asia is as loathsome as in Europe; the Russian miser Plushkin is as pitiable as the French Grandet; the Tartuffes of all countries are alike; misanthropes are equally miserable everywhere, and everywhere every one is equally charmed by the touching image of Don Quixote, the Knight of the Spirit. And after all, all men, in all languages, always speak of the same thing, of themselves and their fate.

Maxim Gorky, 'On literature' (n.d.).

Books are like the windows of a great tower. They let light in.

William Leroy Stidger, *The Place of Books in the Life We Live* (1922).

When we are employed in reading a great and good author, we ought to consider ourselves as searching after treasures, which, if well and regularly laid up in the mind, will be of use to us on sundry occasions in our lives.

Henry Fielding, 'On taste in the choice of books' (n.d.).

I think, consciously or not, what we readers do each time we open a book is to set off on a search for authenticity. We want to get closer to the heart of things, and sometimes even a few good sentences contained in an otherwise unexceptional book can crystallize vague feelings, fleeting physical sensations, or, sometimes, profound epiphanies.

Maureen Corrigan, *Leave Me Alone: I'm Reading* (2005).

But it is not less true that there are books which are of that importance in a man's private experience, as to verify for him the fables of Cornelius Agrippa, of Michael Scot, or of the old Orpheus of Thrace – books which take rank in our life with parents and lovers and passionate experiences, so medicinal, so stringent, so revolutionary, so authoritative – books which are the work and the proof of faculties so comprehensive, so nearly equal to the world which they paint, that, though one shuts them with meaner ones, he feels his exclusion from them to accuse his way of living.

Ralph Waldo Emerson, 'Books' (1870).

Some books seem like a key to unfamiliar rooms in one's own castle.

Franz Kafka, letter to Oskar Pollak, 9th November 1903.

A book is valued not so much for what it reveals in the realm of pure intellect as for what it reveals of the secret sentiments and feelings of the reader.

Francis Grierson, 'The making of books' (1911).

When a man says he sees nothing in a book, he very often means that he does not see himself in it; which, if it is not a comedy or a satire, is likely enough.

A.W. and J.C. Hare, *Guesses at Truth* (1827).

He had dug the book out of a book-seller's shop in Malta, captivated by its title, and had, since the day of its purchase, gone at it again and again, getting nibbles of golden meaning by instalments, as with a solitary pick in a very dark mine, until the illumination of an idea struck him that there was a great deal more in the book than there was in himself.

George Meredith, *Beauchamp's Career* (1876).

We read, frequently if unknowingly, in quest of a mind more original than our own.

Harold Bloom, *How to Read, and Why* (2000).

But the only important thing in a book is the meaning it has for you; it may have other and much more profound meanings for the critic, but at second-hand they can be of small service to you.

W. Somerset Maugham, *The Summing Up* (1938).

*****

Real happiness lies in the little things, in a bit of gardening work, in the rattle of the teacups in the next room, in the last chapter of a book.

W.N.P. Barbellion diary entry 9th May 1911.

And thus my booke, hath bene so moch my pleasure, and bringeth dayly to me more pleasure and more, that in respect of it, all other pleasures, in very deede, be but trifles and troubles vnto me.

Lady Jane Grey, quoted by Roger Ascham, *The Scholemaster* (1571).

I depend on books to help me out when I'm stuck. I dive between the covers of a novel, my foldaway house that travels in my pocket, my cool tent that I can put up wherever and whenever I choose.

Michèle Roberts, *The Book of Mrs Noah* (1987).

As for myself, I never go away from home that I do not take a trunkful of books with me, for experience has taught me that there is no companionship better than that of these friends, who, however much of all things else may vary, always give the same response to my demand upon their solace and their cheer. My sister, Miss Susan, has often inveighed against this practice of mine, and it was only yesterday that she informed me that I was the most exasperating man in the world.

Eugene Field, *The Love Affairs of a Bibliomaniac* (1896).

When the mind is empty of those things that books can alone fill it with, then the seven devils of pettiness, frivolity, fashionableness, gentility, scandal, small slander and the chronicling of small beer come in and take possession.

George Dawson, 'Inaugural address, on the opening of the Birmingham Free Reference Library' (1866).

There is, or there was, an idea that reading in itself is a virtuous and holy deed. I can't quite agree with this, because it seems to me that the mere fact of a man's being fond of reading proves nothing one way or the other.

Rudyard Kipling, 'The uses of reading' (1912).

And, after all, reading is not in itself a virtue; it is only one way of passing the time; talking is another way, watching things another. Bacon says that reading makes a full man; well, I cannot help thinking that many people are full to the brim when they reach the age of forty, and that much which they afterwards put into the over-charged vase merely drips and slobbers uncomfortably down the side and foot.

A.C. Benson, 'Books' (1906).

* * * * *

Books are companions even if you don't open them.

Benjamin Disraeli, letter to Lady Bradford, 29th August 1878.

4. 'TREAT PERSONAL BOOK RECOMMENDATIONS WITH THE SUSPICION THEY DESERVE'

How the mood for a book sometimes rushes upon one, either one knows not why, or in consequence, perhaps, of some most trifling suggestion. Yesterday I was walking at dusk. I came to an old farm-house; at the garden gate a vehicle stood waiting, and I saw it was our doctor's gig. Having passed, I turned to look back. There was a faint afterglow in the sky beyond the chimneys; a light twinkled at one of the upper windows. I said to myself, *Tristram Shandy*, and hurried home to plunge into a book which I have not opened for I dare say twenty years.

George Gissing, *The Private Papers of Henry Ryecroft* (1903).

For a greater part of one's lifetime some books can be like ships that pass in the night. We meet them casually from time to time. Either because their appearance is so distinctive, or their name so striking, we get to know their outward selves quite well. The time comes when no more than a glance, even from a distance, is necessary to tell us what volume it is. Closer examination confirms our guess. The thrill of recognition becomes in time a friendly hail. We acquire quite a lot of information about our chance acquaintance while still remaining aloof. At last the day arrives when opportunity and inclination lead us to go on board.

Oliver Edwards, 'To kill the Count' (1957).

Surely the real way to enjoy a book is not to run after it, but to let it find you. This has been my own method, and although it has kept me for years from knowing certain books, the friendship became much closer than if I had pushed for an introduction in the early days of their existence, when everyone was clamouring about them.

Anonymous, 'Books read on Christmas Day' (1922).

There are certain books that you attempt again and again, and which continue to resist you because you are not ripe for them. During the last twenty years, for instance, I have tried perhaps ten times to read *The Brothers Karamazov* and each time given up in a rage directed equally at Karamazov and myself. Only recently I tried it once more and found its reputation thoroughly deserved. Reading it now with the greatest absorption, I am convinced it is the sort of book that requires the reader (that is, most readers) to be of a certain age. Until now I was simply too young for it, and that's why it seemed to me dull and far-fetched. It is a book you (I mean myself) have to grow up to. One of these days I am going to re-read Turgenev's *Fathers and Sons*, which I raced through at fifteen, getting, I am sure, precisely nothing from it. I have the feeling that I am now about ready for it. But I may be mistaken; I may still be too young for it.

Clifton Fadiman, *Reading I've Liked* (1946).

*****

As for Play-books and Romances, and idle Tales, I have already shewed in my *Book of Self-Denyal*, how pernicious they are, especially to youth, and to frothy, empty, idle wits, that know not *what a man is*, nor what he hath to do in the world. They are powerful baits of the Devil, to keep more necessary things out of their minds, and better Books out of their hands, and to poyson the mind so much the more dangerously, as they are read with more delight and pleasure.

> Richard Baxter, *A Christian Directory: or, A Summ of Practical Theologie, and Cases of Conscience, Directing Christians how to Use their Knowledge and Faith; How to Improve all Helps and Means, and to Perform all Duties; How to Overcome Temptations and to Escape or Mortifie Every Sin* (1678).

Ada had a great stock of books. A few romances, which she read with every appearance of enjoyment, gurgles of laughter erupting from the black bombazine like a hot spring from volcanic earth. But she preferred penny dreadfuls, which she read propped up against the milk bottle as she prepared the evening meal. Fingerprints, translucent with butter, encrusted with batter, sticky with jam, edged every page. Bloody thumbprints led up to one particularly gory murder. All the books had murders in them, all carried out by women. Aristocratic ladies ranged abroad, pushing their husbands into rivers, off balconies, over cliffs, under trains or, in the case of the more domestically inclined, feminine type of woman, remained at home and jalloped them to death. Only the final pages were free of cooking stains and for a long time this puzzled him, until he realized that, in the final chapter, the adulteresses were caught and punished. Ada had no truck with that. *Her* heroines got away with it.

> Pat Barker, *The Ghost Road* (1995).

I admit a liking for novels where something happens.

> Theodore Roosevelt, *A Book-Lover's Holiday in the Open* (1916).

There was a sweet pretty river walk we used to take in the evening and mark the mountains round glooming with a deeper purple; the shades creeping up the golden walls; the river brawling, the cattle calling, the maids and chatterboxes round the fountains babbling and bawling; and several times in the course of our sober walks we overtook a lazy slouching boy, or hobbledehoy, with a rusty coat, and trousers not too long, and big feet trailing lazily one after the other, and large lazy hands dawdling from out the tight sleeves, and in the lazy hands a little book, which my lad held up to his face, and which I dare say so charmed and ravished him, that he was blind to the beautiful sights around him; unmindful, I would venture to lay any wager, of the lessons he had to learn for to-morrow; forgetful of mother waiting supper, and father preparing a scolding; – absorbed utterly and entirely in his book.

What was it that so fascinated the young student, as he stood by the river shore? Not the *Pons Asinorum*. What book so delighted him, and blinded him to all the rest of the world, so that he did not care to see the apple-woman with her fruit, or (more tempting still to the sons of Eve) the pretty girls with their apple cheeks, who laughed and prattled round the fountain! What was the book? Do you suppose it was Livy, or the Greek grammar? No; it was a NOVEL that you were reading, you lazy, not very clean, good-for-nothing, sensible boy! It was D'Artagnan locking up General Monk in a box, or almost succeeding in keeping Charles the First's head on. It was the prisoner of the Château d'If cutting himself out of the sack fifty feet under water (I mention the novels I like best myself – novels without love or talking, or any of that sort of nonsense, but containing plenty of fighting, escaping, robbery, and rescuing) – cutting himself out of the sack, and swimming to the island of Monte Cristo. O Dumas! O thou brave, kind, gallant old Alexandre! I hereby offer thee homage, and give the thanks for many pleasant hours. I have read thee (being sick in bed) for thirteen hours of a happy day, and had the ladies of the house fighting for the volumes. Be assured that the lazy boy was reading Dumas (or I will go so far as to let the reader here pronounce the eulogium, or insert the name of his favourite author); and as for the anger, or it may be, the reverberations of this schoolmaster, or the remonstrances of his father, or the tender pleadings of his mother that he should not let the supper grow cold – I don't believe the scapegrace cared one fig. No! Figs are sweet, but fictions are sweeter.

William Makepeace Thackeray, 'On a lazy idle boy' (1869).

'But you never read novels I dare say?'
'Why not?'
'Because they are not clever enough for you; gentlemen read better books.'
'The person, be it gentleman or lady, who has not pleasure in a good novel must be intolerably stupid. I have read all Mrs Radcliffe's works, and most of them with great pleasure. The *Mysteries of Udolpho*, when I had once begun it, I could not lay down again; I remember finishing it in two days, my hair standing on end the whole time.'

Jane Austen, *Northanger Abbey* (1818).

Plots are for graveyards. I'd rather drag my eyeballs along barbed wire than read a plotty novel. You can almost see authors of such contrived claptrap winding up their childish prose toys, before sending them whirring across their fatuous pages in search of 'adventures'.

Jeff Torrington, *Swing Hammer Swing* (1992).

*****

There are books which are Dinosaurs – Sir Walter Raleigh's *History of the World*, Gibbon's *Decline and Fall of the Roman Empire*.

W.N.P. Barbellion, diary entry 8th July 1914.

I do not believe myself quite alone in my love of the elaborate and the minute; and yet I doubt if many people contemplate very long very big books with the sense of coming enjoyment which such a prospect gives me; and few shrink, as I do, with aversion and horror from that invention of the enemy – an Abridgement.

Mary Russell Mitford, *Recollections of a Literary Life; or, Books, Places and People* (1851).

Long works are too often like long sermons which end in fatigue.

Francis Grierson, 'The making of books' (1911).

The best book for a desert island is Dumas' *Memoirs*. It is the best book for a desert island for various reasons that may as well be tabulated – (a) it is so long that by the time the end was reached either a ship would have arrived or the beginning would be fresh again; (b) it does not matter where you take it up – one page is as good as another, if not better; (c) it requires on the part of the reader no intellectual activity, a plant probably of slow growth amid the tropical luxuries of South Sea isolation; and (d) – and this should of course be (a) – Dumas wrote it.

E.V. Lucas, 'On reading aloud' (1909).

For a desultory reader the anthology is the gateway to literary ecstasy.

William Darling, *The Bankrupt Bookseller* (1931).

Prolixity and dullness become recommendations to a book when you have to consume time, and what is really beautiful, or of use, is received with tenfold gratitude and pleasure.

Robert Southey, letter to Anna Seward, 18th April 1808.

For Continental travel I should myself recommend *Daniel Deronda*. You ought to have a book, and it should be a good book and a long book, and a tolerably dull book. There should be no temptation to turn away from looking at the scenery and resorting to your book, and yet when you wish to turn away there should be something to reward you. There should be no excitement in the narrative to draw you on to the end, but a quiet, steady, easy, unengrossing progress. There are also novels which are adapted only for reading in railway tunnels, but of these I shall not attempt a list.

W. Robertson Nicoll, *A Bookman's Letters* (1913).

There is talk of disseminating the works of our best authors at a cheap rate, in the hope that they will drive the Penny Dreadful out of the market . . . But perhaps the full enormity of the cant about Penny Dreadfuls can best be appreciated by travelling to and fro for a week between London and Paris and observing the books read by those who travel with first-class tickets. I think a fond belief in Ivanhoe-within-the-reach-of-all would not long survive that experiment.

Arthur Quiller-Couch, 'The poor little Penny Dreadful' (1894).

I despair of ever laying aside the reading of trifling books. What I begin I must end.

Henry Crabb Robinson, diary entry 27th February 1824.

I think we ought to read only the kind of books that wound and stab us. If the book we're reading does not wake us up with a blow on the head, what are we reading if for? So that it will make us happy, as you write? Good Lord, we would be happy precisely if we had no books, and the kind of books that make us happy are the kind we could write our-selves if we had to. But we need the books that affect us like a disaster, that grieve us deeply, like the death of someone we loved more than ourselves, like being banished into forests far from everyone, like a suicide. A book must be the axe for the frozen sea inside us. That's my belief.

Franz Kafka, letter to Oskar Pollack, 27th January 1904.

* * * * *

I know people who read the same book over and over again. It can only be that they read with their eyes and not with their sensibility. It is a mechanical exercise like the Tibetan's turning of a prayer wheel. It is doubtless a harmless occupation, but they are wrong if they think it an intelligent one.

W. Somerset Maugham, *The Summing Up* (1938).

I have been clearing my shelves of novels over the past 10 years and survivors are those I wish to reread. That means Dickens, thought I shall be confining myself to my favourites (including *Great Expectations*, which I read every November, for reasons I have yet to fathom).

Paul Bailey, 'Treasure trove' (2004).

There is no doubt that whatever amusement we may find in reading a purely model novel, we have rarely any artistic pleasure in re-reading it. And this is perhaps the best rough test of what is literature and what is not. If one cannot enjoy reading a book over and over again, there is no use in reading it at all.

Oscar Wilde, 'The decay of lying' (1891).

We cannot read the same works forever. Our honeymoon, even though we wed the Muse, must come to an end; and is followed by indifference, if not by disgust. There are some works, those indeed that produce the most striking effect at first by novelty and boldness of outline, that will not bear reading twice: others, of a less extravagant character, and that excite and repay attention by a greater nicety of details, have hardly interest enough to keep alive our continued enthusiasm. The popularity of the most successful writers operates to wean us from them, by the cant and fuss that is made about them, by hearing their names everlastingly repeated, and by the number of ignorant and indiscriminate admirers they draw after them.

William Hazlitt, 'On the pleasure of hating' (1826).

A man who has ceased to take an interest in contemporary literature admits his incapacity to deal with vital questions; he is in the grip of old age; there is no more certain sign of mental decrepitude than chronic denial.

Francis Grierson, 'The past and present' (1911).

*****

It is good to be now and then withheld from reading bad books.

Henry Crabb Robinson, diary entry 28th December 1821.

For among Good Books there are some *very good* that are sound and lively and some are good, but mean, and weak, and somewhat dull: and some are *very good* in parts, but have mixtures of error, or else of incautelus injudicious expressions, fitter to puzzle, than edifie the weak. I am loth to name any of these later sorts (of which abundance have come forth of late).

Richard Baxter, *A Christian Directory: or, A Summ of Practical Theologie, and Cases of Conscience, Directing Christians how to Use their Knowledge and Faith; How to Improve all Helps and Means, and to Perform all Duties; How to Overcome Temptations and to Escape or Mortifie Every Sin* (1678).

I have never had much patience with the writers who claim from the reader an effort to understand their meaning. You have only to go to the great philosophers to see that it is possible to express with lucidity the most subtle reflections.

W. Somerset Maugham, *The Summing Up* (1938).

I, for example, do not react eagerly to books on the delights of gardening; to novels about very young men lengthily and discursively in love; to amateur anthropologists who hide a pogrommania under learned demonstrations of the superiority of Nordic man; to books by bright children Who Don't Know How Funny They're Being; to diplomatic reminiscences by splendid gaffers with long memories and brief understandings; to autobiographies by writers who feel that to have reached the age of thirty-five is an achievement of pivotal significance; to thorough jobs on Chester A. Arthur; to all tomes that aim to make me a better or a more successful man than I would be comfortable being; to young, virile novelists who would rather be found dead than grammatical; to most anthologies of humour; to books about Buchmanism, astrology, Yogi, and internal baths, all of which seem to me to deal with the same subject matter as does the last of the four subjects named; to the prospect of further 'country' books, such as *Country Mortician*, *Country Dog-Catcher*, and *Country Old Ladies' Home Attendant*.

Clifton Fadiman, *Reading I've Liked* (1946).

Books, I fancy, may be conveniently divided into three classes:

1. Books to be read, such as Cicero's *Letters*, Suetonius, Vasari's *Lives of the Painters*, the *Autobiography of Benvenuto Cellini*, Sir John Mandeville, Marco Polo, St Simon's *Memoirs*, Mommsen, and (till we get a better one) Grote's *History of Greece*.

2. Books to be re-read, such as Plato and Keats: in the sphere of poetry, the masters not the minstrels; in the sphere of philosophy, the seers not the *savants*.

3. Books not to be read at all, such as Thomson's *Seasons*, Roger's *Italy*, Paley's *Evidences*, all the Fathers except St Augustine, all John Stuart Mill except *Essay on Liberty*, all Voltaire's plays without any exception, Butler's *Analogy*, Grant's *Aristotle*, Hulme's *England*, Lewes's *History of Philosophy*, all argumentative books and all books that try to prove anything.

Oscar Wilde, letter to the Pall Mall Gazette, 1886.

Even the most indifferent of biographies is more readable than most novels.

William Darling, The Bankrupt Bookseller (1931).

For me, as for many others, the reading of detective stories is an addiction like tobacco or alcohol. The symptoms of this are: firstly, the intensity of the craving – if I have any work to do, I must be careful not to get hold of a detective story for, once I begin one, I cannot work or sleep till I have finished it. Secondly, its specificity – the story must conform to certain formulas (I find it very difficult, for example, to read one that is not set in rural England). And, thirdly, its immediacy. I forget the story as soon as I have finished it, and have no wish to read it again. If, as sometimes happens, I start reading one and find after a few pages that I have read it before, I cannot go on.

W.H. Auden, 'The guilty vicarage' (1963).

I still read a great deal of criticism, for I think it is a very agreeable form of literary composition. One does not always want to be reading to the profit of one's soul and there is no pleasanter way of idling away an hour or two than by reading a volume of criticism. It is diverting to agree; it is diverting to differ; and it is always interesting to know what an intelligent man has to say about some writer, Henry More, for instance, or Richardson, whom you have never had occasion to read.

W. Somerset Maugham, *The Summing Up* (1938).

The normal, healthy reader will no more stick at one book for, say, a fortnight, than he will eat nothing but Quaker Oats for the same period. If he reads a Historian in the morning, he will want an Essayist in the afternoon, and a Poet at night. No one is better worth reading than Gibbon, but a month devoted to *Decline and Fall* with no excursions into other spheres, no parleyings with other writers, might lead to a surfeit of the book, and a quarrel with the author.

Frederick Macdonald, *Recreations of a Book-Lover* (1911).

*****

I cannot wax enthusiastic about Readers Union choice for September. Probably because my mind has been so occupied with more topical matters, I could work up no deep interest in the life of William the Silent.

George Taylor, diary entry 24th September 1945.

To me the heading employed by some reviewers when they speak of 'books of the week' comprehensively damns both the books themselves and the reviewer who is willing to notice them. I would much rather see the heading 'books of the year before last'. A book of the year before last which is still worth noticing would probably be worth reading; but one only entitled to be called a book of the week had better be tossed into the wastebasket at once.

Theodore Roosevelt, *A Book-Lover's Holiday in the Open* (1916).

I think authors do not sufficiently bear in mind the important fact that, in this age of ours, the public *thinks for itself* much more intensively than we give it credit for. It is a cultured public, and its great brain is fully capable of deciding things. It rather objects to be treated like a child and told 'what to read and what to avoid'; and moreover, we must not fail to note that it mistrusts criticism generally, and seldom reads 'reviews'. And why? Simply because it recognises the existence of 'logrolling'. It is perfectly aware, for instance, that Mr Theodore Watts is logroller-in-chief to Mr Swinburne; that Mr Gallienne 'rolls' greatly for Mr Norman Gale; and that Mr Andrew Lang tumbles his logs along over everything for as many as his humour fits.

> Marie Corelli, quoted by Arthur Quiller-Couch,
> 'The attitude of the public towards letters' (1894).

But the difficulty of choosing the books which are to adorn the shelves is now almost insuperable, unless current literature is to be excluded altogether. The degradation of reviewing, since it became tacitly if not expressly venal, leaves the willing reader and buyer to make his choice unguarded. He dare not risk the exasperation which follows when the recommendation of what he took to be a reliable and competent judge turns out to have been nothing but a piece of professional or personal toadying.

> Arthur Goidel, 'Books' (1946).

*****

To me, no present is so acceptable as a book on Christmas morning, if it happens to be one that has not before come my way. Long ago I had a friend who for years gave me a book on Christmas Day. Sometimes it was a book costing five shillings, or seven and sixpence; sometimes it was only a shilling reprint. But always it was welcome, because always it was a book that I had not read before, carefully selected by a man who knew my tastes and had some acquaintance with the books on my shelves. The memory of that Christmas packet, and the pleasurable anticipations it aroused, is grateful to look back on.

Anonymous, 'Books read on Christmas Day' (1922).

A long time ago when he and Diana were courting they had had an embittered argument about Diana's response, or rather lack of response, to the Russian novelists. Diana, in fact, read a lot but that particular taste of his he had not been able to transmit. He had said, in a fit of annoyance in a pub in Charlotte Street, 'If you want to go through life as a person who's never read *The Possessed* then that's your problem.' Diana, quite justifiably as he now considered, had got up and walked out and he had had to pursue her into Tottenham Court Road and embark on a reconciliation outside Goodge Street station.

Penelope Lively, *According to Mark* (1984).

Usually, of course, I treat personal book recommendations with the suspicion they deserve. I've got enough to read as it is, so my first reaction when someone tells me to read something is to find a way to doubt their credentials, or to try to dredge up a conflicting view from the memory. (Just as stone always blunts scissors, a lukewarm 'Oh, it was OK', always beats a 'You have to read this.' It's less work that way.)

Nick Hornby, *The Complete Polysyllabic Spree* (2006).

5. 'THE PLEASANT THING IS . . .':

The time and place for a book

I must confess even now a partiality for a handsome Globe of gold-fish – then I would have it hold 10 pails of water and be fed continually fresh through a cool pipe with another pipe to let through the floor – well ventilated they would preserve all their beautiful silver and Crimson – Then I would put it before a handsome painted window and shade it all round with myrtles and Japonicas. I should like the window to open onto the Lake of Geneva – and there I'd sit and read all day like the picture of somebody reading.

John Keats, letter to Fanny Keats, 13th March 1819.

I was staying with an uncle at Canterbury for the Christmas holidays; it was a snowy afternoon and, going by chance into a bookshop, I found three thick little volumes in a binding new to me, the first volumes I was told of a wonderful new series. They were cheap, they were thick, they were seductive; the series was named 'The World's Classics,' and the three volumes that I then purchased and took home with me were Hazlitt's *Essays*, Poe's *Tales* and Poems by Keats. I went back to the warm, thickly-curtained library and sat over the fire. My uncle's house abutted on the Cathedral, and as I read the organ was rumbling and humming as though it were in the very room with me. Although I could not see it, I knew that the snow was falling thickly beyond the windows; in the next room they were hanging holly over the pictures. I think almost any book in the world would have been entrancing to me that afternoon, but when I began 'On Going a Journey'

and passed from that to 'The Indian Jugglers' I knew a rich-
ness of satisfaction that was quite astounding in its surprise.

Hugh Walpole, *These Diversions: Reading* (1926).

But the pleasant thing is to wake early, throw open the
window, and lie reading in bed.

Edward Fitzgerald, letter to W.F. Pollock, 3rd May 1840.

I then return to my own room to breakfast. I make this
meal the most pleasant part of the day; I have a book for my
companion, and I allow myself an hour for it.

Fanny Burney, diary entry 24th July 1786.

Who cannot recall, as I can, the reading they did in the holidays, which one would conceal successively in all those hours
of the day peaceful and inviolable enough to be able to afford
it refuge. In the mornings, after returning from the park, when
everyone had gone out for a walk, I would slip into the dining-
room, where no one would be coming until the still distant
hour for lunch except for the old, relatively silent, Félicie, and
where I would have for my sole companions, most respectful
of reading, the painted plates hanging on the wall, the calen-
dar from which the previous day's page had been newly torn,
the clock and the fire, which speak but without demanding
that one answer them and whose quiet remarks are void of
meaning and do not, unlike human speech, substitute a different meaning for that of the words you are reading. I would
settle myself on a chair, near the small log fire of which, during
lunch, my early rising uncle, the gardener, would say: 'That
doesn't do any harm! I can put up with a bit of fire; it was jolly
cold in the vegetable garden at six o'clock I can assure you.
And to think it's only a week to Easter!' Before lunch, which
would, alas, put a stop to my reading, lay two whole hours.

Marcel Proust, 'Days of reading (1)' (1905).

The evenings are a little chilly out-of-doors; but the days are glorious. I rise before seven; breakfast at nine; write a page; ramble five or six hours over rocks and through copsewood, with Plutarch in my hand; come home; write another page; take Fra Paolo, and sit in the garden reading till the sun sinks behind the Undercliff. Then it begins to be cold; so I carry my Fra Paolo into the house and read on till dinner. While I am at dinner the Times comes in, and is a good accompaniment to a delicious dessert of peaches, which are abundant here. I have also a novel of Theodore Hook by my side, to relish my wine. I then take a short stroll by starlight, and go to bed at ten. I am perfectly solitary; almost as much as Robinson Crusoe before he caught Friday. I have not opened my lips, that I remember, these six weeks, except to say 'Bread, if you please,' or 'Bring a bottle of soda water'; yet I have not had a moment of ennui.

Thomas Babington Macaulay, letter to
T.F. Ellis, 8th September 1850.

I almost always read a good deal in the evening; and if the rest of the evening is occupied I can at least get half an hour before going to bed. But all kinds of odd moments turn up during even a busy day, in which it is possible to enjoy a book; and then there are rainy afternoons in the country in autumn, and stormy days in winter, when one's work out-doors is finished and after wet clothes have been changed for dry, the rocking chair in front of the open wood-fire simply demands an accompanying book.

Theodore Roosevelt, *A Book-Lover's Holiday in the Open* (1916).

Dad's book was propped against the teapot. Maura sat on his right with her book open against the sugar basin and Kate, crammed on his left between the sideboard and the dining table, had her book balanced against the cruet set.

Her mother sat out in the kitchen with her books and pamphlets spread among the pots on the Formica table. From time to time she called, 'Want any more?' and if they answered yes, preoccupied, turning a page, there would be a rustling of paper before she appeared bearing a saucepan and the big spoon. The fire burned in the grate; the radio played 'Popular Parade': 'How Much is that Doggie in the Window?' *(wuff wuff)*.

Fiona Farrell, *Book Book* (2004).

Mother's predecessor had left behind him a large number of Yellow Backs. These still lay where they had been found, on the top shelf of the outdoor bathroom; and to get at them necessitated a climb, with one foot balanced precariously on the edge of the bath. I managed it one Saturday night, which was hot-bath night, when I was allowed to take my time. A sort of Roman bath I made of it, with a plate of fruit and cake on a chair beside me, and one of those novels in my hands. Here I read *Lady Audley's Secret*, *Aurora Floyd*, and various others, including one called *The New Magdalen*, over which I had seen my elders purse their lips.

Henry Handel Richardson, *Myself When Young* (1948).

Raymond Petitjacques lay neatly tucked up in his bed, indulging in his secret vices: he was munching on a chocolate praline, of which a whole box stood on his bedside table, and reading Alexandre Dumas' *The Three Musketeers*.

Arthur Koestler, *The Call Girls: A Tragi-Comedy* (1973).

Matilda would visit the library only once a week in order to take out new books and return the old ones. Her own small bedroom now became her reading-room and there she would sit and read most afternoons, often with a mug of hot chocolate beside her. She was not quite tall enough to reach things around the kitchen, but she kept a small box in the outhouse which she brought in and stood on in order to get whatever she wanted. Mostly it was hot chocolate she made, warming the milk in a saucepan on the stove before mixing it. Occasionally she made Bovril or Ovaltine. It was pleasant to take a hot drink up to her room and have it beside her as she sat in her silent room reading in the empty house in the afternoons.

Roald Dahl, *Matilda* (1988).

She read, at peace with the world and happy as only a little girl could be with a fine book and a bowl of candy, and all alone in the house.

Betty Smith, *A Tree Grows in Brooklyn* (1943).

Having locked her door, Virginia made certain preparations which had nothing to do with natural repose. From the cupboard she brought out a little spirit-kettle, and put water to boil. Then from a more private repository were produced a bottle of gin and a sugar-basin, which, together with a tumbler and spoon, found a place on a little table drawn up within reach of the chair where she was going to sit. On the same table lay a novel procured this afternoon from the library. Whilst the water was boiling, Virginia made a slight change of dress, conducive to bodily ease. Finally, having mixed a gin and water – one-third only of the diluent – she sat down with one of her frequent sighs, and began to enjoy the evening.

George Gissing, *The Odd Women* (1893).

I've got a shelf full of books with HMP Pentonville, HMP Wandsworth on them, smuggled 'em out, yeah. *Crime and Punishment* I read! Except my cellmate at the time kept on pulling his shorts down and getting his knob out, and going, 'Is this normal, Pete?' And I'm trying to read.

Pete Doherty, quoted in *The Guardian*, 3rd October 2006.

Books which we have first read in odd places always retain their charm, whether read or neglected . . .Haphazard meetings with books sometimes present them under conditions hopelessly unfavourable, as when I encountered Whitman's *Leaves of Grass* for the first time on my first voyage in an Azorian barque; and it inspires to this day a slight sense of nausea, which it might, after all, have inspired equally on land.

Thomas Wentworth Higginson, 'Books unread' (1904).

He disappeared rather in a panic during a two-days' gale, in which he had the portholes of his cabin battened down, and remained in his cot reading the 'Washerwoman of Finchley Common', left on board the Ramchunder by the Right Honourable the Lady Emily Hornblower, wife of the Reverend Silas Hornblower, when on their passage out to the Cape, where the Reverend gentleman was a missionary: but, for common reading, he had brought a stack of novels and plays which he lent to the rest of the ship, and rendered himself agreeable to all by his kindness and condescension.

William Makepeace Thackeray, *Vanity Fair* (1848).

Anna arranged herself with pleasure and deliberation for the journey. With small, deft hands she opened a red bag and took a little cushion, which she laid on her knees before relocking the bag. Then she carefully wrapped a rug round her legs and sat down again. An invalid lady had already settled herself for the night. Two other ladies began talking to Anna, and a stout old woman tucked up her feet and remarked upon the heating of the train. Anna said a few words in reply, but, not foreseeing any entertainment from the conversation, asked Annushka to get a lamp, hooked it on the arm of her seat, and took a paper-knife and an English novel from her bag.

Leo Tolstoy, *Anna Karenin* (1876).

I have certainly spent some enviable hours at inns . . . I might mention luxuriating in books, with a peculiar interest in this way, as I remember sitting up half the night to read Paul and Virginia, which I picked up at an inn at Bridgewater, after being drenched in the rain all day; and at the same place I got through two volumes of Madame D'Arblay's Camilla. It was on the tenth of April 1798, that I sat down to a volume of the New Eloise, at the inn at Llangollen, over a bottle of sherry and a cold chicken. The letter I chose was that in which St Preux describes his feelings as he first caught a glimpse from the heights of the Jura of the Pays de Vaud, which I had brought with me as a *bonne bouche* to crown the evening with.

William Hazlitt, 'On going a journey' (1821).

Xenagorabibliomania – an obsessive curiosity about the books that strangers read in open spaces.

Nick Hornby, 'Can't put it down?' (2006).

But when I lived much in cow camps I often carried a volume of Swinburne, as a kind of antiseptic to alkali dust, tepid, muddy water, frying-pan bread, sow-belly bacon, and the too-infrequent washing of sweat-drenched clothes.

Theodore Roosevelt, *A Book-Lover's Holiday in the Open* (1916).

After breakfast I got my air mattress and retrieved Thomas Mann from my knapsack. I wandered off a few hundred feet, out of sight of the mess and pup tents, and entered into a thin pine forest, pine needles on a forest floor exactly like the one where the earth moved for Maria and Robert Jordan in *For Whom the Bell Tolls* – Professor Flanagan's course; this would have been March 1954 – and settled the air mattress against a tree at precisely the angle where my helmet would make a comfortable pillow for my head.

It moved for me, too. I had picked a spot at the very edge of the trees, with a view of the passes and mountains beneath me wide as beauty. It moved for me too. I could have been the only man in the world. It moved and moved.

I opened my book and began to read 'Mario the Magician'. It was, to then, the most wonderful story I'd ever read, the finest ever written. Or maybe it was the circumstances, maybe it was the day.

Stanley Elkin, *Pieces of Soap* (1992).

The born reader reads anywhere, anywhen, by day or night, by the light of the moon and the stars, or even, so I have heard, by lightning or the *aurora borealis*; by sunlight and candlelight, gaslight or electricity; on land or sea, walking or riding, standing or sitting or lying in bed; on chairs or sofas, on couches, in hammocks, in baths and at stool; on board ships, in punts, rowing-boats, and canoes; up trees; on ladders; on omnibuses, or bicycles, in railway trains, or automobiles, cabs, carriages, tramway cars, jaunting cars, buggies, balloons, airships or aeroplanes, or any other vehicle for sea, land or air; in hospitals, penitentiaries, prisons; in kitchens, parlours, caves, arbours, etc.; on the backs of horses, camels, mules, asses, elephants; in hot and cold climates, in all countries and all places; in houses, hotels, theatres, mines, concert halls, submarines, bar-parlours, saloons, billiard-rooms, turkish baths, sun-boxes, pastry cooks', barbers' shops, waiting-rooms at railway stations; in the ante-rooms of Ministers of State, and the waiting-rooms of physicians, surgeons, dentists, etc.; in churches during service, surreptitiously and not always the *Holy Word*; in law courts; in streets walking or standing or leaning against a wall; in fields or forests; on the *Underground* in London, the *Overhead* in Liverpool, and the *El* at New York, regardless of noise; during air raids and bombardments, wars, revolutions and pestilences; in joy and sorrow, health and sickness.

Holbrook Jackson, *The Anatomy of Bibliomania* (1930).

6. 'THE GOOD PRACTICE OF BUYING A BOOK A DAY'

But is there any substance to the plaint that nobody now buys books, meaning thereby second-hand books? The late Mark Pattison, who had 16,000 volumes, and whose lightest word has, therefore, weight, once stated that he had been informed, and verily believed, that there were men of his own University of Oxford who, being in uncontrolled possession of annual incomes of not less than £500, thought they were doing the thing handsomely if they expended £50 a year upon their libraries. But we are not bound to believe this unless we like. There as a touch of morosity about the late Rector of Lincoln which led him to take gloomy views of men, particularly Oxford men.

Augustine Birrell, 'Book buying' (1905).

Gentle book-hunting is a pleasant occupation. To amble idly through the second-hand shops with a watchful, hopeful, but by no means anxious or purposeful eye; to be delighted if, by any chance, after 20 years of searching one does come across a copy of Trollope's *Marion Fay* or *Castle Richmond*, the second volume of Kirke White's *Remains*, or of John Stuart Mill's *Three Essays on Religion*; to be almost equally happy to come out with nothing at all – these are delights for a questing but a quiet mind. Patience is everything. The years are long; we are in no hurry; there is plenty to read meanwhile. And if the day ever does come when, going up or down stairs in Cambridge, or Edinburgh, or Guildford, or Tunbridge Wells, we suddenly come face to spine with Godwin's *Mandeville* then the pleasure will be all the greater because the encounter has to wait half a lifetime.

Oliver Edwards, 'Mock laurel' (1957).

Sometimes books were arranged under signs, but sometimes they were just anywhere and everywhere. After I understood people better, I realized that this incredible disorder was one of the things that they loved about Pembroke Books. They did not come there just to buy a book, plunk down some cash and scram. They hung around. They called it browsing, but it was more like excavation or mining. I was surprised they didn't come in with shovels. They dug for treasures with bare hands, up to their armpits sometimes, and when they hauled some literary nugget from a mound of dross, they were much happier than if they had just walked in and bought it. In that way shopping at Pembroke was like reading: you never knew what you might encounter on the next page – the next shelf, stack or box – and that was part of the pleasure of it.

Sam Savage, *Fermin* (2007).

The trouble with bookshops is that they are as bad as pubs. You start with one and then you drift to another, and before you know where you are you are on a gigantic book-binge. My brief case was full to bursting and I had bundles of books under both arms. I was bowed down by the weight of them.

R.T. Campbell, *Bodies in a Bookshop: A Detective Story* (1946).

Marguerite came back last night from 2 days in Paris, and brought 2 books – new, French, fresh as fruit. Astonishing the pleasure of merely contemplating them as they lay on the table. I must really, once settled in Fontainebleau, resume the good practice of buying a book a day.

Arnold Bennett, diary entry 18th March 1908.

In those times, Cooke's edition of the British poets came up. I had got an odd volume of Spencer; and I fell passionately in love with Collins and Gray. How I loved those little six-penny numbers containing whole poets! I doted on their size; I doted on their type, on their ornaments, on their wrappers containing lists of other poets, and on the engravings from Kirk. I bought them over and over and over again, and used to get up select sets, which disappeared like buttered crumpets; for I could resist neither giving them away, nor possessing them. When the master tormented me – when I used to hate and loathe the sight of Homer, and Demosthenes, and Cicero – I would comfort myself with thinking of the sixpence in my pocket, with which I should go out to Paternoster Row, when school was over, and buy another number of an English poet.

Leigh Hunt, Autobiography (1850).

The most discouraging feature of the mania for book-collecting is, that it grows by what it feeds on, and becomes the more insatiable the more it is gratified.

William Mathews, Hours with Men and Books (1877).

Do you remember the brown suit, which you made to hang upon you, till all your friends cried shame upon you, it grew so thread-bare – and all because of that folio Beaumont and Fletcher, which you dragged home late at night from Barker's in Covent-garden? Do you remember how we eyed it for weeks before we could make up our minds to the purchase, and had not come to a determination till it was near ten o'clock of the Saturday night, when you set off from Islington, fearing you should be too late – and when the old bookseller with some grumbling opened his shop, and by the twinkling taper (for he was setting bedwards) lighted out the relic from his dusty treasures – and when you lugged it home, wishing it were twice as cumbersome – and when you presented it to me – and when we were exploring the perfectness of it (*collating* you called it) – and while I was repairing some of the loose leaves with paste, which your impatience would not suffer to be left till day-break – was there no pleasure in being a poor man?

Charles Lamb, 'Old china' (1823).

'And here's the Charing Cross Road. This is where all the second-hand book shops are. Many's the hour I've spent poking about in some of these places; standing, sometimes, for the whole of lunch time, reading some book I couldn't afford to buy. Yes, you can stand there as long as you like, reading, and no-one says a word.'

Emily heard his words with something of a thrill. She determined to avail herself at the first opportunity of the facilities of this enlightened, courteous street.

John Collier, *His Monkey Wife* (1930).

You will love London which, amid its grey-gold haze, with the red smudges of its motor-buses and the dark smudges of its policemen, is like a huge Turner. You will love its theatres with their comfortable stalls, pretty attendants, and short intervals. You will love its book-shops, appetising and multi-coloured as its shops full of exotic fruits, and especially you will love the books . . . only say it not.

André Maurois, 'Advice to a young Frenchman
starting for England' (1929).

But what were even gold and silver, precious stones and clockwork, to the bookshops, whence a pleasant smell of paper freshly pressed came issuing forth, awakening instant recollections of some new grammar at school, long time ago, with 'Master Pinch, Grove House Academy,' inscribed in faultless writing on the fly-leaf! That whiff of russia leather, too, and all those rows on rows of volumes, neatly ranged within: what happiness did they suggest! And in the window were the spick-and-span new works from London, with the title-pages, and sometimes even the first page of the first chapter, laid wide open: tempting unwary men to begin to read the book, and then, in the impossibility of turning over, to rush blindly in, and buy it!

Charles Dickens, *Martin Chuzzlewit* (1843–4)

Many a time and oft one rejects a book with disdain because of an attempt to force its purchase. Our English friends have learned the art of skilful innuendo. When you take from its resting-place on the shelf some precious volume which causes the heart to palpitate, and timidly enquire the price, they almost apologize for even mentioning such a thing. Experiences like these brighten the life of a book-lover.

Adrian Joline, *Diversions of a Book-Lover* (1903).

Certain stall-keepers have a jealousy of order which they would do well to moderate. An amateur may not have finished investigating a box in which he has looked at a book which he has not carefully put back in its place, when the dealer is at his side, picking out the volumes, dusting them with his sleeve, and arranging them in a new way as if to purify them from contamination.

Octave Uzanne, *The Book-Hunter in Paris* (1893).

*****

'Davie Wilson,' he said, 'commonly called Snuffy Davie, from his inveterate addiction to black rappee, was the very prince of scouts for searching blind alleys, cellars, and stalls, for rare volumes. He had the scent of a slow-hound, sir, and the snap of a bull-dog. He would detect you an old black-letter ballad among the leaves of a law-paper, and find an *editio princeps* under the mask of a school Corderius. Snuffy Davy bought the *Game of Chess*, 1474, the first book ever printed in England, from a stall in Holland, for about two groschen, or twopence of our money. He sold it to Osborne for twenty pounds, and as many books as came to twenty pounds more. Osborne resold this inimitable windfall to Dr Askew for sixty guineas. At Dr Askew's sale,' continued the old gentleman, kindling as he spoke, 'this estimable treasure blazed forth in its full value, and was purchased by Royalty itself, for one hundred and seventy pounds!'

Walter Scott, *The Antiquary* (1816).

. . . the others push past him, with like informality, down the step, and dive directly into separate areas of the shop. Naturally they ignore the books on the few remaining shelves, or those in what might once have been a glass-fronted cabinet – but immediately start to examine, with painstaking care, the loose sheets under the tables, anything without a spine; they spill out the contents of boxes onto the floor.

'All crap,' Dryfeld announces, unnecessarily.

'You guys!' Mossy remarks, world-weary, but with something of admiration in this tone. 'You fucking guys.'

He succeeded in spearing a spectacularly colourful gob of snot and prodded it across the counter. It was speckled like granite. He'd probably have it set into a signet ring.

'You're too fucking much.' He killed a bottle of room temperature Lucozade, spun open the cap on another.

Dryfeld, totally ignoring the prices inscribed in the books, which bore no relation to their value, at auction, by catalogue, or any other method of trade known to humanity, started to put a heap of 'possibles' on the counter, 'for negotiation.' He's quite prepared to talk it through to dawn;

or until the first shop opens in Hendon. Or until Mossy's screaming cells demand another anodyne fix. Whoever talked about getting high hadn't met Mossy. He absorbed, sweated, continued. He looked like an ill-shaved bison but he had a will that could only be measured in geological time. His stock might need carbon dating, but he wouldn't crack.

First edition dealers are interested in nothing but condition, they couldn't care less about the title or the contents so long as the book is fine, mint, untouched, intact, a second time virgin: they wouldn't have a prayer here.

But Nicholas Lane is resilient, he starts to work through a mess of *Horner's Penny Stories for People*, so well-tanned they're oven ready; pausing to examine one copy closely. He hasn't blinked since they got out of the car: his pupils enlarge by a couple more points. He snatches up the whole pile, putting them under his arm. Then rapidly selects a hand of terminally distressed Austin Freemans, a 'Lost Race' yarn, lacking front free endpaper, a romance set in Burma, and a Jonathan Latimer paperback for his own use. Nicholas Lane and Dryfeld were remarkable figures in the book trade: they could both read, a book a day, between shops. The speed of Lane's decisions was breathtaking and those who know him will recognize that he has made a find. All of the other choices are wrapping paper and can be painlessly junked.

The Late Watson is somewhat languid. The shop looks uncomfortably like a diagram of his stomach. He began to hallucinate. The room extended into the dreadnought hulk of Ripon Cathedral. It was raining, or the roof was melting. The pews were stacked with untitled proof copies, a thousand to every row, and somewhere in amongst them Graham Greene's own copy, the original version, of *Brighton Rock*, with all the period racism not yet expurgated. He needed to run his head under a tap. He blundered through the main body of the shop, up some steps, into the back room.

The bowl of the lavatory was filled with painted female faces. Titles like *Blue Blood Flows East, Lady – Don't Turn Over*, floated sodden on the surface. The Science Fiction titles were spread over the floor, along with a good supply of used and unused needles. Crunch across them, like walking on locusts. There is no light, he has a torch in his pocket, ready for winter morning markets, for nipping into forbidden cellars and peeping through the keyholes of locked rooms. Spots a tolerable copy of *The Anubis Gates* by Tim Powers, published 1985 at £9.95 and modestly marked up by Mossy to £15. That's ok. He can get £40 for it. Picks up half a dozen others to jettison when they negotiate. Back to the shop, one sleeper, an inscribed copy of Peter Ackroyd's *Hawksmoor* for a fiver: which brings him up to his day's target.

The sole advantage of Mossy's shop is that he does not offer coffee to dealers. This form of politeness has wrecked more stomachs than the combined forces of all the fast food dead-chicken combos.

'You're putting me on, man. This lot comes to £238 – I'm saying you can have them for £210. Two hundred. And ten. Pounds. What do you want, man, me to *give* them to you? For Chrissakes, man!'

Mossy's indignation is perfectly assumed, almost genuine. He falls back, breathless.

Dryfield, unmoved. '£60. Best offer.'

'Get out of here! You know what they catalogue at? Are you *serious*?'

'Sixty quid. Take it or leave it.'

'I'm giving you nearly three hundred fucking quids worth of books, where else in this world are you even going to *see* these books? Giving, at £200. What do you want? Bastard! You want to fuck my wife and kids as well?'

'Sixty quid.'

Iain Sinclair, *White Chappell, Scarlet Tracings* (1987).

One day I was in this shp and made an offer for a firework bk that had been there for at least a year. First the assistant acted as it I had done something unmentionable, and then went off in search of reassurance from the owner. Meanwhile I paced up and down, rebrowsing, assistant came back and asked if he heard me correctly, but by this time I was thinking of reading the book & using it & began re-rebrowsing. Ten minutes later assistant reappeared, how much was I thinking of offering. I decreased the amount I had thought of by 20% as aggravation tax, assistant then disappears. As I was re-re-rebrowsing I noticed a book which had nothing on the spine & took it off the shelf. It was marked £1. I smiled, eventually assistant reappears. I hardly recognized him, he seemed so much older. I'm awfully sorry Sir, but the proprietor says we don't take offers. I gave him the £1 and left. Outside I woke my friend in the car and offered him the book for fifty, he offered £40, I almost declined. He asked £80 from somebody else and got offered £70 the same day. I can never understand this thing about offers. I look upon the price as the one chance a bookdealer gets to use his imagination.

B.C.M. Driffield, *All the Secondhand and*
Antiquarian Bookshops (1986).

The bookshop was in the Butts, by the church, a musty, galleried building full of mildewed volumes that no one would ever read again. The young assistant seemed dubious about adding to them, and took the books from Angel, glanced at them and shrugged his shoulders. 'I'll enquire,' he said. When he came back, he was smiling with false pity. 'No, I'm afraid we should have no use for them. We could offer one and sixpence.'

'Two shillings,' Angel said, burning with humiliation.

'Now, come,' he said insolently. 'You don't want to make me go all the way back and ask again for the sake of sixpence.'

'Yes, I do.'

He sighed extravagantly, but he went away and when he came back it was without the books. He handed her the florin with infuriating solemnity and, as she turned to leave the shop, called after her: 'Don't spend it all at once, will you?'

'You ill-bred jackanapes!' Angel said loudly. He looked startled, but when she turned to close the door she could see him through the glass panel. He was bowed over the counter, as if weeping or in pain: for a moment she felt appeased, and then she saw that he was convulsed with laughter.

Elizabeth Taylor, *Angel* (1957).

He was toting a Braniff Airlines flight bag in one ill-manicured hand and the Everyman's Library edition of *The Poems of William Cowper* in the other.

He set the book down next to the cash register, reached into a pocket, found two quarters, and placed them on the counter alongside the book.

'Ah, poor Cowper,' I said, picking up the book. Its binding was shaky, which was why it had found its way to my bargain table. 'My favourite's "The Retired Cat". I'm pretty sure it's in this edition.' He shifted his weight from foot to foot while I scanned the table of contents. 'Here it is. Page one-fifty. You know the poem?'

'I don't think so.'

'You'll love it. The bargain books are forty cents or three for a dollar, which is even more of a bargain. You just want the one?'

'That's right.' He pushed the two quarters an inch or so closer to me. 'Just the one.'

'Fine,' I said. I looked at his face. All I could really see was his brow, and it looked untroubled, and I would have to do something about that. 'Forty cents for the Cowper, and three cents for the Governor in Albany, mustn't forget him, and

what does that come to?' I leaned over the counter and daz-
zled him with my pearly-whites. 'I make it thirty-two dollars
and seventy cents,' I said.

'Huh?'

'That copy of Byron. Full morocco, marbled end papers,
and I believe it's marked fifteen dollars. The Wallace Stevens
is a first edition and it's a bargain at twelve. The novel you
took was only three dollars or so, and I suppose you just
wanted to read it because you couldn't get anything much
reselling it.'

'I don't know what you're talking about.'

I moved out from behind the counter, positioning myself
between him and the door. He didn't look as though he
intended to sprint but he was wearing running shoes and you
never can tell. Thieves are an unpredictable lot.

'In the flight bag,' I said. 'I assume you'll want to pay for
what you took.'

'This?' He looked down at the flight bag as if astonished
to find it dangling from his fingers. 'This is just my gym stuff.
You know – sweat socks, a towel, like that.'

'Suppose you open it.'

Perspiration was beading on his forehead but he was trying
to tough it out. 'You can't make me,' he said, 'You've got no
authority.'

'I can call a policeman. He can't make you open it either,
but he can walk you over to the station house and book
you, and *then* he can open it, and do you really want that to
happen? Open the bag.'

He opened the bag. It contained sweat socks, a towel, a
pair of lemon-coloured gym shorts, and the three books I had
mentioned along with a nice clean first edition of Steinbeck's
The Wayward Bus, complete with dust wrapper. It was
marked $17.50, which seemed a teeny bit high.

'I didn't get that here,' he said.

'You have a bill of sale for it?'

'No, but –'

I scribbled briefly, then gave him another smile. 'Let's call it fifty dollars even,' I said, 'and let's have it.'

'You're charging me for the Steinbeck?'

'Uh-huh.'

'But I had it with me when I came in'

'Fifty dollars,' I said.

'Look, I don't want to *buy* these books.' He rolled his eyes at the ceiling. 'Oh God, why did I have to come in here in the first place? Look, I don't want any trouble.'

'Neither do I.'

'And the last thing I want to buy is anything. Look, keep the book, keep the Steinbeck too, the hell with it. Just let me get out of here, huh?'

'I think you should buy the books.'

'I don't have the money. I got fifty cents. Look, keep the fifty cents too, okay? Keep the shorts and the towel, keep the sweat socks, okay? Just let me get the hell out of here, okay?'

'You don't have any money?'

'No, nothing. Just the fifty cents. Look –'

'Let's see your wallet.'

'What are you – I don't have a wallet.'

'Right hip pocket. Take it out and hand it to me.'

'I don't believe this is happening.'

I snapped my fingers. 'The wallet.'

It was a nice enough black pinseal pinfold, complete with the telltale outline of a rolled condom to recall my own lost adolescence. There was almost a hundred dollars in the currency compartment. I counted out fifty dollars in fives and tens, replaced the rest, and returned the wallet to the owner.

'That's my money,' he said.

'You just bought the books with it,' I told him. 'Want a receipt?'

'I don't even want the books, dammit.' His eyes were watering behind the thick glasses. 'What am I going to do with them, anyway?'

'I suppose reading them is out. What did you plan to do with them originally?'

He stared at his track shoes. 'I was going to sell them.'

'To whom?'

'I don't know. Some store.'

'How much were you going to get for them?'

'I don't know. Fifteen, twenty dollars.'

'You'd wind up taking ten.'

'I suppose so.'

'Fine,' I said. I peeled off one of his tens and pressed it into his palm. 'Sell them to me.'

'Huh?'

'Saves running from store to store. I can use good books, they're the sort of item I stock, so why not take the ten dollars from me?'

'This is crazy.'

'Do you want the books or the money? It's up to you.'

'I don't want the books.'

'Do you want the money?'

'I guess so.'

I took the books from him and stacked them on the counter. 'Then put it in your wallet,' I said, 'before you lose it.'

'This is the craziest thing ever. You took fifty bucks from me for books I didn't want and now you're giving me ten back. I'm out forty dollars, for God's sake.'

'Well, you bought high and sold low. Most people try to work it the other way around.'

'*I* should call a cop. I'm the one getting robbed.'

Lawrence Block, *The Burglar Who Liked to Quote Kipling* (1979).

Secretly, the Scotchman hated bookdealers, and as he sold to them, he exacted a terrible revenge. He razored out, with unusual care, one page from the middle of the text, so delicately, it was never noticed. The books were passed on, shelved, never read. In many of the great collections were books that had been emasculated and were valueless. The Scotchman liked that. It made him feel good. It never came back on him. Thinking about it, he smiled.

Iain Sinclair, *White Chappell, Scarlet Tracings* (1987).

*****

Jack Hack was interested in the book department, believing in some mysterious way that it added grace and intellect to the store. In the old days, according to a theory of the time, books and stationery and art goods had been neighboured together at the rear of the main floor. The philosophy of this arrangement was rational enough. Silk stockings and gloves and other feminine trifles put the customer in a mood of sentiment. Sentiment suggests correspondence, and one was imperceptibly in the stationery department. Writing paper led logically towards the idea of reading; reading dissolved into paint-boxes and the graphic arts, which in turn developed into toys.

But in a hopeful mood the Hacks has been persuaded that their literary patrons would appreciate more privacy. Books were not just ordinary merchandise, they were assured; they need to be examined in leisure and along comfortable shelves. Calculations were even advanced as to the likelihood of customers getting backache from bending over tables to look at the volumes. In a flush of idealism Hack Brothers installed the book department in a quadrangle of its own. Here secluded alcoves were furnished with rugs and armchairs and glass cases of fine bindings. Toys and Art Materials were shifted up to the Sporting Goods floor; only Literature's wistful consort, Stationery, still lingered near her cloistered partner. Books, so to speak, had taken the veil, but just outside the shrine the worldly sister remained faithful, consoling herself with samples of nuptial engraving in which Mr and Mrs Gunsaulus Bendix announced the marriage of their daughter Margaretta Beulah to Mr Einar Tastrom.

There were fallacies in this theory of segregating the book department. In the first place, it is dangerous, in the shopping arena, to give women an opportunity to sit down. Mr Hack observed with pain that Milady (that phantom of the millinery world) was using the literary alcoves as a rest-room or rendezvous rather than as a place of purchase. Over the archway that led to the department a high-minded architect had painted, in Gothic letters, the legend BOOKS ARE FRIENDS THAT NEVER AGE. This, after the next ensuing Mark-Down Sale, was found to be so obviously untrue that Mr Hack replaced it by the sturdy and prosaic statement, in electric bulbs, ENTRANCE TO THE BOOK DEPARTMENT.

Another thought might have occurred to the Hack Brothers if they had known more about the matter. It is over falbalas and fanfreluches, not books, that women desire to linger and loiter and exercise the spasms of choice. In regard to books they have usually made up their minds beforehand; they know exactly what they want. ('Don't miss it, my dear.') And they enjoy the bustle and colour of the open aisles; enjoy the skirmish of many rivals pressing forward with eager toddle, alert faces turning this way and that like foraging poultry. To their quick humour it is all the fun of a social event without the strain of having to be polite. The quiet backwater of the book department frightens them just a little. – But the book department had one great advantage, daylight on street frontage. Mrs Beaton and her clerks were never so indignant as when a customer from within the main store would come pressing through, disregarding their zealous display of Latest Fiction, merely to verify in daylight the colour of some gay foulard. It was hard then for plump and mettlesome little Beaton not to be able to say, with just the right sardonic tone, 'And may I interest you in a little Literature?'

Christopher Morley, *Human Being* (1932).

Given a good pitch and the right amount of capital, any educated person ought to be able to make a small secure living out of a bookshop. Unless one goes in for 'rare' books it is not a difficult trade to learn, and you start at a great advantage if you know anything about the insides of books.

George Orwell, 'Bookshop memories' (1936).

Gretel, who worked in a bookshop, had helped Jachin-Boaz find a job as an assistant in another shop. His salary was small and the owner was delighted with him. There was about Jachin-Boaz an aura of seeking and finding that customers responded to. People who for years had not looked for things in books found new appetites for knowledge when they spoke to him. To someone who came in asking for the latest novel he might sell not only the novel but a biological treatise on the life of ants, an ecological study of ancient man, a philosophical work, and a history of small sailing-craft.

Russell Hoban, *The Lion of Boaz-Jachin and Jachin-Boaz* (1973).

He took me to an old bookseller's named Lehec, in the rue St André des Arts. We could scarcely get into the shop for books. Lehec told us he had a hundred thousand; the place smelt of damp paper. He was an oldish thin man, wearing a hat and a black smock like a French child's pinafore.

I wanted a good edition of *The Memoirs of Fanny Hill*. He had a copy upstairs in his flat. He took us up, in the dark, to the third storey, and having opened the door made us enter

quickly lest his cat should escape. When he had struck a light
we saw the cat – a superb Persian. A curiously arranged flat,
small, very clean bourgeois . . . Here again was all books. He
at last, after searching through several portmanteaus full of
bawdy English books, found a fine edition of *Fanny Hill* in
two volumes.

Arnold Bennett, diary entry 14th December 1904.

London bookshops, from the little I know of them, are either
austere or dirty, with one or two austere and dirty. The most
palladian of them all is Quaritch's, a single sumptuous book
in each window. Wanted very much to go in there last time I
was in town, but hardly liked to without a definite book to ask
for. Supposing I had marched in and inquired if they possessed
a 1725 edition of Bellenger's *Dispute on the Conduct of the
Papacy* with erratum leaf, or some such title conjured up on
the moment's spur: could I be sure that my subconscious had
not played me false, and that such a book did not exist?

'Certainly, sir,' the man in the frock coat would say. 'On
the third floor; we will ascend in the lift. We can offer you
two copies of the 1725 edition, one in original boards from
the library of the Earl of Divan and Dungeness and one in full
vellum with Bellenger's signature on the flyleaf. Or we have
the much rarer 1723 edition, which as you know lacks sub-
title and dedication.

'We also possess Bellenger's short tract *Et Nunc Manet
in Mensam Reginae*, which he wrote when tutor to Milord
Happisburgh, price £125.'

And as in a horrible dream, instead of extricating myself
quickly and coming away – saying perhaps I'd wait till
Penguins reprinted it – I should try and save face, and pretend I was writing the life of Lord Happisburgh. Before I
knew it, I should be staring thunderstruck at a portfolio full
of unpublished documents relating to the Happisburghs from

Tudor times to the War of Jenkins' Ear.

'I'd better come back tomorrow,' I should say. 'I've forgotten my reading-glasses.'

'Certainly, sir. We will reserve the documents for you meanwhile, in case you should suffer the vexation of finding them purchased in the interim. Would you care to leave your address and the name of your bank?'

'Oh, a postcard care of the Post Office Saving Bank will always reach me,' and with that I should rush, weeping, for the street.

Brian Aldiss, *The Brightfount Diaries* (1955).

You should know that it is considered definitely low-minded to try and buy any kind of a book in Canada, even from a bookseller.

Malcolm Lowry, letter to Maxwell Perkins, 20th September 1946.

*****

Great and liberal is the magic of bookstalls; truly deserved is the title of cheap shops. Your second-hand bookseller is second to none in the worth of the treasure which he dispenses; far superior to most; and infinitely superior in the modest profits he is content with. So much so, that one really feels ashamed sometimes to pay him such nothings for his goods. In some instances (for it is not the case with every one) he condescends even to expect to be 'beaten down' in the price he charges, petty as it is; and accordingly, he is good enough to ask more than he will take, as though he did nothing but refine upon the pleasure of the purchaser. Not content with valuing knowledge and delight at a comparative nothing, he takes ingenious steps to make even that nothing less; and under the guise of a petty struggle to the contrary (as if to give you an agreeable sense of your energies) seems dissatisfied unless he can send you away thrice blessed, – blessed with the book, blessed with the cheapness of it, and blessed with the advantage you have had over him in making the cheapness cheaper.

Leigh Hunt, 'Bookstalls and "Galateo"' (1847).

I scarcely ever pass by their boxes without picking out of one of them some old book which I had always been in need of up to that very moment, without any suspicion of the fact on my part.

Anatole France, *The Crime of Sylvestre Bonnard* (1881).

Book hunting was for this academician such a serious function that he wore a special costume for the purpose; he could stow away bundles of books in his pockets, which were numerous and as deep as sacks.

Octave Uzanne, *The Book-Hunter in Paris* (1893).

*****

That one should possess no books beyond his power of perusal – that he should buy no faster than as he can read straight through what he has already bought – is a supposition alike preposterous and unreasonable. 'Surely you have far more books than you can read,' is sometimes the inane remark of the barbarian who gets his books, volume by volume, from some circulating library or reading club, and reads them all through, one after the other, with a dreary dutifulness, that he may be sure that he has got the value of his money.

John Hill Burton, *The Book Hunter* (1863).

. . . a promise postponed for several years – namely, not to buy any more books until I've finished reading the ones arrayed along the Read Next shelf, piled up in the fireplace and stacked semi-neatly on the floor of the sitting room, study, bedroom and kitchen. And on the stairs. And under the bed. You get the idea. Lots of books. Unread.

Lucy Mangan, '2008 – the year I'm gonna get cultured' (2007).

He resolved again, as he had resolved many times, to read nothing but the books he already owned. Really to get to know the Jonson plays; to find quotations from Montaigne rising unbidden to his lips – how inspiring and how economical! He turned and walked with fresh vigour up the slope to Marble Arch.

Roy Fuller, *The Second Curtain* (1953).

7. 'MUDDLING AMONG OLD BOOKS'

I wrote, read and walked with the most stoical regularity.
This muddling among old books has the quality of a sedative
and saves the tear and wear of an overwrought brain.

Walter Scott, diary entry 29th March 1829.

Thence home and dined, and to Deptford and got all my pictures put into wherries, and my other fine things, and landed
them all very well, and brought them home and got Symson
to set them up all tonight; and he gone, I and the boy to finish
and set up my books and everything else in my house, till 2 in
the morning, and then to bed. But mightily troubled, and even
in my sleep, at my missing four or five of my biggest books –
Speed's Chronicle – and maps, and the two parts of Waggoner,
and a book of Cards; which I suppose I have put up with too
much care, that I have forgot where they are, for sure they are
not stole. Two little pictures of sea and ships, and a little gilt
frame belonging to my platt of the River I want; but my books
do heartily trouble me. Most of my gilt frames are hurt, which
also troubles me; but most my books.

Samuel Pepys, diary entry 19th September 1666.

A hideous thing has marked to-day. You must know that
I had chosen and packed with great care some fifty volumes,
to be presently sent to me abroad; well, in the transit to the
warehouse, the box *broke*, and – but it is too loathsome to
talk of. I have been perspiring, gasping, coughing, and trembling all day long. Two more such days, and I should move
into my grave.

George Gissing, letter to H.G. Wells, 21st April 1899.

I had some liabilities and three assets, when I arrived in M---. One of the liabilities was the 70 large volumes of Voltaire printed in Paris in 1784, which socially and psychologically did me no good and materially throughout my six years in India proved a considerable difficulty when they had to be moved over hundreds of miles in a country without railways. I am rather proud of the fact that socially I lived down the 70 volumes and physically brought them back to England in fair conditions neither repudiating Voltaire spiritually and socially nor abandoning him materially.

Leonard Woolf, 'Memoirs of an elderly man' (1945).

Books, books, books!
I had found the secret of a garret-room
Piled high with cases in my father's name,
Piled high, packed large, – where, creeping in and out
Among the giant fossils of my past,
Like some nimble mouse between the ribs
Of a mastodon, I nibbled here and there
At this or that box, pulling through the gap
In heats of terror, haste, victorious joy,
The first book first. And how I felt it beat
Under my pillow, in the morning's dark,
An hour before the sun would let me read!
My books!

Elizabeth Barrett Browning, *Aurora Leigh* (1856).

My father taught all his children to read and write. In the winter when the fishing was over and the storms wrapped Gaze Island, my father would hold school right down there in the kitchen of the old house. Yes, every child on this island learned to read very well and write a fine hand. And if he got a bit of money he'd order books for us. I'll never forget one time, I was twelve years old and it was November 1933. Couple of years before he died of TB. Hard, hard times. You can't imagine. The fall mail boat brought a big wooden box for my father. Nailed shut. Cruel heavy. He would not open it, saved it for Christmas. We could hardly sleep nights for thinking of that box and what it might hold. We named everything in the world except what was there. On Christmas Day we dragged that box over to the church and everybody craned their necks and gawked to see what was in it. Dad pried it open with a screech of nails and there it was, just packed with books. There must have been a hundred books there, picture books for children, a big red book on volcanoes that gripped everybody's mind the whole winter – it was a geological study, you see, and there was plenty of meat in it. The last chapter in the book was about ancient volcanic activity in Newfoundland. That was the first time anybody had ever seen the word Newfoundland in a book. It just about set us on fire – an intellectual revolution. That *this place* was in a book. See, we thought we were all alone in the world. The only dud was a cookbook. There was not one single recipe in that book that could be made with what we had in our cupboards.

E. Annie Proulx, *The Shipping News* (1993).

Here I begin to feel myself at home and am already enough acquainted with the house to go about in the dark; this is the criterion I think of intimacy with a dwelling place. To day my books are to arrive; two windows that have been blocked up on account of the tax form two convenient recesses for them, I have knocked up some shelves there, and when my box arrives from Cottles I shall need no other society.

Robert Southey, letter to John May, 8th July 1798.

I am unpacking my library. Yes, I am. The books are not yet on the shelves, not yet touched by the mild boredom of order. I cannot march up and down their ranks to pass them

in review before a friendly audience. You need not fear any
of that. Instead, I must ask you to join me in the disorder
of crates that have been wrenched open, the air saturated
with wood dust, the floor covered with torn paper, to join me
among piles of volumes that are seeing daylight again after
two years of darkness, so that you may be ready to share with
me a bit of the mood – certainly not an elegiac mood but,
rather, one of anticipation – which these books arouse in a
genuine collector.

> Walter Benjamin, 'Unpacking my library' (1931).

Books, it has already been said, are snobbish. I always
knew that in a vague way, but lately I have had proof of it.
Owing to circumstances – no matter what – my books have
been divided. Some are in town, and others – the bulk – are
in the country. Naturally, those that are in town, where my
daily work lies, are carefully selected; those that are in the
country are a mixture of all sorts. Now, I have discovered
that the books on my town shelves have never changed in
their countenance towards me since I separated them from old
companions; they have, in fact, grown more friendly. Those
in the country, on the other hand, have grown decidedly cold
to me when I pick them up during my week-ends. Especially
is it the case with some that used to be most friendly: the old
rapport is gone. The change is not in me, I am sure; it is in the
books. They are, in fact, sulking.

This may be due to three causes, or one of three. There is,
first of all, my comparative neglect of them. There is no surer
way to estrange friendship of a certain kind than neglect.
And books, being highly sensitive, feel this neglect as much as
persons. They have known familiar friendship, and they will
not give of their best when friendship becomes casual. This is
hard on a man who must have his books in two places, and
only spends one and a half days a week with a number of

them who used to live with him always. But one can understand and respect the delicate proud resentment.

Or it may be to unfavourable conditions. When my books were all together, they were in a beautiful hall in an old-fashioned house. Because they were in so conspicuous a place they had to be properly arranged, and the effect was very grand, almost noble, although there were no more than 2,000 volumes, all told. I could go straight to any shelf and pick out just the book I wanted, just as can be done in real libraries. There was no sulking of friends in those days, although I was then, as now, a week-ender. In fact, I used to think they gave me more as the visitor of Saturday to Monday then they used to give me when they lived all the week with me. Of course, they were by no means neglected in the intervening days. The old dark-stained hall and the 'lovely books' were the objects of much country admiration. But now, in another house, there is no 'noble 'all', and no spare room for books. So they are divided into three groups – in dining-room, in drawing-room, and – the bulk – ranged along the walls of a passage, at the end of which a window opens on the garden. It is a queer fact that the books in the passage are sulking most. An outrage has been put on their dignity by being put in a thoroughfare.

Or it may be that they have uncongenial companionship. Because there is no picturesque hall to show them off, and no book room in which to make an atmosphere, the most of my country books are shoved into shelves, huddled up any way without the remotest attempt at classification. Now, you simply can't treat books that way and expect them to smile at you.

Anonymous, 'The snobbishness of books' (1922).

After a time, libraries settle down. Everyone knows that philosophic air of accepting the situation that creeps over every library after a certain period of discontent. I said every library, but that is too general; there are rooms where one knows at once on entering that discontent is brooding, and that it will always be so. These are rooms in which glaring editions de luxe are laid out on the table, not for reading, but for admiration, and where the latest novel or two are piled beside the easy chair. There is no real love of literature here, no real love of Reading here, and the older books on the bookshelves know it. Owners of such libraries are for ever wondering why things go wrong with their books: volumes disappear, and they suppose it is because dishonest visitors steal them; do they try to move a book from a shelf numbers of other books fall upon their heads, and when they would arrange a volume or two all the books close at hand fall on their backs and lie there sulkily contemptuous. Their library never 'looks right,' they can't tell why; would it not be better if they moved their Poetry *there*, or put Froude and Macaulay (whom they have never bothered as yet to read) on to that shelf over there? No, madam, it will not make the slightest difference; what you have got to change is your Reading Heart, and as you are far too old and self-satisfied for that you had better leave the matter alone.

Horace Walpole, *These Diversions: Reading* (1926).

Last year I almost resolved to become less sentimental about books. Then I was saved, at the 11th hour, by a friend who confessed to me in a drunken state at a New Year's Eve party that her book collection is organised according to which ones she thinks would get on with each other in 'real life'. You know, if they were human. So Portnoy's Complaint is at the opposite end of the room from Pride and Prejudice, because 'he' would bully 'her'. Forever Amber is next to Anya Seaton's Katherine 'obviously', and The Pilgrim's Progress is within hailing distance of His Dark Materials because, although they would be in disagreement over many things, she thinks they would find their conversations mutually rewarding. Not the authors: the books.

This, I felt, was a step change from my predilection for considering my books as close personal friends and spending hours gazing at the covers in reverie, recalling the good times we have had together.

Lucy Mangan, '2008 – the year I'm gonna get cultured' (2007).

Dominie Sampson was occupied, body and soul, in the arrangement of the late bishop's library, which had been sent from Liverpool by sea, and conveyed by thirty or forty carts from the seaport at which it was landed. Sampson's joy at beholding the ponderous contents of these chests arranged upon the floor of the large apartment, from whence he was to transfer them to the shelves, baffles all description. He grinned like an ogre, swung his arms like the sails of a windmill, shouted 'Prodigious' till the roof rang to his raptures. 'He had never,' he said, 'seen so many books together, except in the College Library'; and now his dignity and delight in being superintendent of the collection raised him, in his own opinion, almost to the rank of the academical librarian, whom he had always regarded as the greatest and happiest man on earth . . . He entered them in the catalogue in his best running hand, forming each letter with the accuracy of a lover writing a valentine, and placed each individually on the destined shelf with all the reverence which I have seen a lady pay to a jar of old china. With all his zeal his labour advanced slowly. He often opened a volume when half-way up the library-steps, fell upon some interesting passage, and, without shifting his inconvenient posture, continued immersed in the fascinating perusal until the servant pulled him by the skirts to assure him that dinner waited. He then repaired to the parlour, bolted his food down his capacious throat in squares of three inches, answered aye and no at random to whatever question was asked at him, and again hurried back to the library, as soon as his napkin was removed, and sometimes with it hanging round his neck like a pinafore.

Walter Scott, *Guy Mannering* (1815).

W. Hewer tells me that upon enquiry, he doth find that Sir W. Penn hath a hamper more than his own, which he took for a hamper of bottles of wine, and are books in it. I was impatient to see it, but they were carried into a wine-cellar, and the boy is abroad with him at the House, where the Parliament meet today, and the King to be with them. At noon, after dinner, I sent for Harry, and he tells me it is so, and brought me by and by my hamper of books, to my great joy, with the same books I missed, and three more great ones and no more – I did give him 5s for his pains; and so home with great joy, and to the setting some of them right.

Samuel Pepys, diary entry 21st September 1666.

My ideological position has always been that books should be left to find their own order. The frequently refer-enced will rise to the top; the comfort reads and the ones to which you just like to see and know they are there will find their way naturally to the appropriately prominent shelves. Those you have read only once and know you never will again, drift quietly down to less accessible areas between chairs, behind the computer and under the stairs. Thus, your books will eventually end up arranged in strata that best serve your needs without feeling injured by deliberate relegation or smug thanks to premeditated elevation.

Lucy Mangan, 'I'm alphabetising my books – oh no!' (2007).

On Kate's mother's shelves, books had been catalogued in terms of memory: this section belonged to her youth and her career at Oamaru Public Hospital, this to the time of her marriage, these were her daughters' books (the ones they had left behind), these belonged to her husband. Just as cupboards held cardboard cartons full of old toys, her nurse's cape and stethoscope, receipts dating back to the purchase of the villa in Oamaru in 1948, guarantees for appliances long discarded, and electrical leads, plugs, picture hooks, hanks of string, paper bags neatly folded, Christmas cards and knitting patterns – all the things someone, sometime might want again – so the bookshelves stood as evidence of a life. The books were part of the record.

Fiona Farrell, *Book Book* (2004).

*****

R. and I, both coughing, stay in the library with our log fire. I have begun to dust the books, climbing on the steps in a smock and Pobble-like pink cotton gloves.

Frances Partridge, diary entry 26th January 1940.

I think she found some sort of therapy in dusting bookshelves – taking all the books off, all of them, and Hoovering them. She preferred dusting the books to reading them.

Denis Oliver on Margaret Thatcher, 'Into the void' (2007).

And so, being little to do at the office, did go home; and after spending a little at righting some of my books which stood out of order, I to bed.

Samuel Pepys, diary entry 13th October 1666.

8. 'HE SPOILS EVERY DECENT BOOK ON WHICH HE LAYS HIS HANDS'

All men are not as considerate of books as I am; I wish they were. Many times I have felt the deepest compassion for noble volumes in the possession of persons wholly incapable of appreciating them. The helpless books seem to appeal to me to rescue them.

Eugene Field, *The Love Affairs of a Bibliomaniac* (1896).

My pet foe is the individual who turns the corners of the leaves, who drags the book from the shelf by the top, and who lays it open face downward.

Adrian Joline, *The Diversions of a Book-Lover* (1903).

There is a right way and a wrong way of taking a book from the shelf. To put a finger on the top, and so extract the volume by brutal leverage, is a vulgar error which has broken many backs. This was never his way: he would gently push back each of the adjacent books, and so pull out the desired volume with a persuasive finger and thumb. Then, before opening the pages, he applied his silk handkerchief on the gilded top, lest dust should find its way between the leaves.

R.W. Chapman, 'The portrait of a scholar' (1920).

His library was famous. Dealers had often besieged him for unique editions. Perhaps she was planning some vast robbery. He must find out how she acted when she was alone with the book.

One day he surprised her in the kitchen. His doubts tormented him; he longed for certainty. Once unmasked, he would throw her out. He wanted a glass of water; she had evidently not heard him calling. While she made haste to satisfy his wishes, he examined the table at which she had been sitting. On a small embroidered velvet cushion lay his book. Open at page 20. She had not yet read very far. She offered him the glass on the plate. It was then he saw that she had white kid gloves on her hands. He forgot to close his fingers round the glass; it fell to the floor, the plate after it. Noise and diversion were welcome to him. He could not have brought a word to his lips. Ever since he was five years old, for thirty-five years, he had been reading. And the thought had never once crossed his mind, to put on gloves for the purpose.

Elias Canetti, *Auto da Fé* (1935).

In the first place as to the opening and closing of books, let there be due moderation, that they not be unclasped in precipitate haste, nor when we have finished our inspection be put away without being duly closed. For it behoves us to guard a book much more carefully than a boot.

But the race of scholars is commonly badly brought up, and unless they are bridled in by the rules of their elders they indulge in infinite puerilities. They behave with petulance, and are puffed up with presumption, judging of everything as if they were certain, though they are altogether inexperienced.

You may happen to see some headstrong youth lazily lounging over his studies, and when the winter's frost is sharp, his nose running from the nipping cold drips down, nor does he think of wiping it with his pocket-handkerchief until he has bedewed the book before him with the ugly moisture. Would that he had before him no book, but a cobbler's apron! His nails are stuffed with fetid filth as black as jet, with which he marks any passage that pleases him. He distributes a multitude of straws, which he inserts to stick out in different places, so that the harm may remind him of what his memory cannot retain. These straws, because the book has no stomach to digest them, and no one takes them out, first distend the book from its wonted closing, and at length, being carelessly abandoned to oblivion, go to decay.

He does not fear to eat fruit or cheese over an open book, or carelessly to carry a cup to and from his mouth; and because he has no wallet at hand he drops into books the fragments that are left. Continually chattering, he is never weary of disputing with his companions, and while he alleges a crowd of senseless arguments, he wets the book lying half open in his lap with sputtering showers. Aye, and then hastily folding his arms he leans forward on the book, and by a brief spell of study invites a prolonged nap; and then, by way of mending the wrinkles, he folds back the margin of the leaves, to the no small injury of the book.

Now the rain is over and gone, and the flowers have appeared in our land. Then the scholar we are speaking of, a neglecter rather than an inspector of books, will stuff his volume with violets, and primroses, with roses and quatrefoil. Then he will use his wet and perspiring hands to turn over the volumes; then he will thump the white vellum with gloves covered in all kinds of dust, and with his fingers clad in long-used leather will hunt line by line through the page; then at the sting of the biting flea the sacred book is flung aside, and is hardly shut for a month, until it is so full of the dust that has found its way within, that is resists the effort to close it.

But the handling of books is specially to be forbidden to those shameless youths, who as soon as they have learned to form the shapes of letters, straightway, if they have the opportunity, become unhappy commentators, and wherever they find an extra margin about the text, furnish it with monstrous alphabets, or if any frivolity strikes their fancy, at once their pen begins to write it. There the Latinist and sophister and every unlearned writer tries the fitness of his pen, a practice that we have frequently seen injuring the usefulness and value of the most beautiful books.

Again, there is a class of thieves shamefully mutilating books, who cut away the margins from the sides to use as material for letters, leaving only the text, or employ the leaves from the ends, inserted from the protection of the book, for various uses and abuses – a kind of sacrilege which should be prohibited by the threat of anathema.

Again, it is part of the decency of scholars that whenever they return from meals to their study, washing should invariably precede reading, and that no grease-stained finger should unfasten the clasps, or turn the leaves of a book. Nor let a crying child admire the pictures in the capital letters, lest he soil the parchment with wet fingers: for a child instantly touches whatever he sees. Moreover, the laity, who look at a book turned upside down just as if it were open in the right way, are utterly unworthy of any communion with books.

Ricardi de Bury, *Philobiblon* (1345).

You remember how I used to stuff bread, and fill the book I was reading with crumbs? I dare say the old Euripides is bulging out with them now.

Leigh Hunt, 'Jack Abbott's breakfast' (1847).

But few book-ghouls are worse than the moral ghoul. He defaces, with a pen, the passages, in some precious volume, which do not meet his idea of moral propriety. I have a Pine's 'Horace', with the engravings from gems, which has fallen into the hands of a moral ghoul. Not only has he obliterated the verses which hurt his delicate sense, but he has actually scraped away portions of the classical figures, and 'the breasts of the nymphs in the brake.'

Andrew Lang, *The Library* (1881).

Many people, it seems, are convinced that the front end-paper – the blank page at the beginning of a book – exists to be written on. Ladies and gentlemen, the free endpaper is not there to scribble on, otherwise, as it used to say on computer cards when computers used cards, 'tear, fold, spindle or mutilate'. The endpaper has the same significance in a book as the silences in a Pinter play, the gaps between movements in a Beethoven quartet or the unpainted canvas of one of Bacon's screaming popes. Between the gaudiness of the dust wrapper and the solemnity of the text, it provides a beat.

Rupert Croft-Cooke, *English Cooking: A New Approach* (1960).

I didn't intend to come back for a very long time, if at all, so, instead of packing a lot of things to sell, I took on board a pretty large trunk full of books. I gave them most of Plato, even more of Aristotle, and Theophrastus's work on botany – but this, I'm sorry to say, was in rather poor condition, as I'd carelessly left it lying around while we were at sea, and a monkey had got hold of it. He amused himself by playfully ripping out odd pages here and there, and tearing them to pieces.

Thomas More, *Utopia* (1516).

But there was mastery in destroying the books. I would first tear off the covers, then rip the pages out in clumps. I would cut each page into long strips and feed them to the blender. When they emerged they were like Michaelmas-daisies. I would stow them away in large plastic bags and weekly, I would leave the shredded offerings down on the street below, to be collected by dustmen. They would lie there beside the other bulging bags of tins, cartons, uneaten dinners and soggy tea-leaves. My bags were pristine, clean, and pure as a child in a christening robe. I would imagine their journey, mangled and crushed in the grinding, toothed lorry, smeared with the wretched saliva of household refuse, to be tipped out at the large dump by an angry, white-capped sea. Perhaps one or two pieces would remain unsullied, only to be haggled over by peevish seagulls, themselves the only white, clear beings on a landscape of greying, disintegrating humanity.

Mary Morrissy, 'Bookworm' (1993).

'That's the story about me in Marygreen, is it – that I entrapped 'ee? Much of a catch you were, Lord send!' As she warmed she saw some of Jude's dear ancient classics on a table where they ought not to have been laid. 'I won't have them books here in the way!' she cried petulantly; and seizing them one by one she began throwing them on the floor.

'Leave my books alone!' he said. 'You might have thrown them aside if you had liked, but as to soiling them like that, it is disgusting!' In the operation of making lard Arabella's hands had become smeared with hot grease, and her fingers consequently left very perceptible imprints on the book-covers. She continued deliberately to toss the books severally upon the floor, till Jude, incensed beyond bearing, caught her by the arms to make her leave off. Somehow, in doing so, he loosened the fastening of her hair, and it rolled about her ears.

'Let me go!' she said.

'Promise to leave the books alone.'

She hesitated. 'Let me go!' she repeated.

'Promise!'

After a pause: 'I do.'

Thomas Hardy, *Jude the Obscure* (1895).

I have a fear upon me least Coleridge should get at my books, and carry any of them off with him: for in the first place he spoils every decent book on which he lays his hands, and in the next place the moment it is in his hands he considers it to all intents and purposes as his own, and makes no scruple of bescrawling it, of giving it away – in short of doing any thing with it, except taking care of it and returning it to its owner.

> Robert Southey, letter to Charles Danvers, 20th April 1807.

While I think on it, Coleridge, I fetch'd away my books which you had at the *Courier* Office, and found all but a third volume of the old plays, containing the *White Devil*, Green's *Tu Quoque*, and the *Honest Whore*, perhaps the most valuable volume of them all – *that* I could not find. Pray, if you can, remember what you did with it, or where you took it out with you a walking perhaps; send me word, for, to use the old plea, it spoils a set.

> Charles Lamb, letter to Samuel Taylor Coleridge, June 1809.

Letters have been pouring in in shoals (please notice that when it is a question of shoals of letters, they always pour) regarding the book-handling service inaugurated by my Dublin WAAMA League. It has been a great success. Our trained handlers have been despatched to the homes of some of the wealthiest and most ignorant in the land to maul, bend, bash and gnaw whole casefuls of virgin books. Our printing presses have been turning out fake Gate Theatre and Abbey programmes by the hundred thousand, not to mention pamphlets in French, holograph letters signed by George Moore, medieval playing cards, and the whole paraphernalia of humbug and pretence.

There will be a black sheep in every fold, of course. Some of our handlers have been caught using their boots, and others have been found thrashing inoffensive volumes of poetry with horsewhips, flails, and wooden clubs. Books have been savagely attacked with knives, daggers, knuckle-dusters, hatchets, rubber-piping, razor-blade-potatoes, and every device of assault ever heard of in the underworld. Novice handlers, not realising that tooth-marks on the cover of a book are not accepted as evidence that its owner has read it, have been known to train terriers to worry a book as they would a rat. One man (he is no longer with us) was sent to a house in Kilmainham, and was later discovered in the Zoo handing in his employer's valuable books to Charlie the chimpanzee. A country-born handler 'read' his books beyond all recognition by spreading them out on his employer's lawn and using a horse and harrow on them, subsequently ploughing them in when he realized he had gone a little bit too far. Moderation, we find, is an extremely difficult thing to get in this country.

Flann O'Brien, 'Book handling' (n.d.).

Collectors abominate lending libraries. They are graveyards of good books. Everything a librarian does to prepare a book for lending disqualifies it as a collectable. Stamps are slammed on the title page, label pockets gummed to the rear pastedown, dust wrappers discarded, covers vulcanized in plastic – or, in those days, a toffee-brown buckram tough enough to withstand acid. Restoring a library book to collectable condition is like trying to return a Kentucky Fried Chicken to the state of health where it can lay an egg.

John Baxter, A Pound of Paper (2002).

I am in the back room of the library, listening to a donated CD of Scott Joplin rags on our miserable portable CD player, trying to put a pile of damaged best sellers back together armed only with rubber cement and a hot glue gun designed for home crafters on a budget. It is a regular job, a job that has to be done, though not necessarily by me. A patron comes in to check out a hot new best seller, takes it home, puts it on his nightstand, and opens it up later when day is done. The book opens a little stiffly, because it is new and has never been opened before. The pages are crisp and bright white, and the cover is shiny, ummottled so far by coffee rings or trips to the beach. The patron gets comfortable in bed and opens up the book – it opens tentatively – and the patron bends the open book backwards until there is a satisfying crack and the book is a little more supple, a little easier to read. The book spine has just been broken, and a broken spine means a more submissive book.

Immediately, the physics of the book are changed. It begins to slop and lean against itself, one way or another, when it is closed. It drifts from a rectangular shape to more of a rhomboid. A small section of interior pages begins to bulge out past the hardboard cover as if it were going to seed, and these pages will tatter and discolour, eventually separating themselves completely from the rest of the book.

A broken spine in a book, especially in a public library, means the book is beginning to die. This was more rare ten or fifteen years ago, and is more common now when every aspect of a book is judged by its profitability, and the ingredients in the printing processes are often of a lesser quality.

Rubber cement and hot glue – and me, incidentally – combine for an inexpensive, last-ditch effort to save a mass-market hardback book. It gives the book one last chance to be read by a few more people, if they are careful. The library knows that it is a temporary fix. We have a stamp for the inside of the front cover: BROKEN SPINE NOTED. It is like a bracelet worn by a diabetic. When you return the book with the message stamped inside, we know you're not the one responsible for this horrible thing. It was some other bastard before you. The book has a pre-existing condition.

Don Borchert, *Library Confidential* (2007).

Got some more red enamel paint (red, to my mind, being the best colour), and painted the coal scuttle, and the backs of our *Shakespeare*, the binding of which had almost worn out.

George and Weedon Grossmith, *The Diary of a Nobody* (1892).

Second-hand books in good condition I will put up with if need be; they are so much cheaper, and there is no avoiding them when new copies are out of stock or out of print. But whether the edition is the first or the tenth, whether the title-page or the paper wrapper is missing or the original binding has been changed interests me as little as whether my cigarettes came from a packet or a box. A first folio Shakespeare seems to me to be no more worth having than the first velocipede; the same thing can be had in a much handier and more pleasing shape.

Arthur Goidel, 'Books' (1946).

Occasionally, however, I found a book which, even in terrible condition, was too desirable to discard. Truman Capote's first short-story collection, for example, was something I simply had to have, even though the catalogue entry of the copy I ferreted out of a junk shop would have read:

CAPOTE, Truman. A TREE OF NIGHT AND OTHER STO-
RIES, William Heinemann, London, 1950. First British
printing. Lacks dust wrapper. Original green cloth
bumped at all corners. Cloth faded to a blotched rust
colour around all margins of front and back boards,
and along spine, which is also sunned. Large stamps
on front pastedown and front free endpaper. ('SECOND-
HAND BOOKS, STAMPS AND MAGIC, City Centre Arcade,
Penrith. Bought, Sold, Exchange'). Small bookseller's
label on front pastedown. Figure $2' in ballpoint on
front pastedown. Illegible signature and date on front

free endpaper. Fore-edges, prelims, and first pages of
text forged . . .

Everything, in short, but a used condom for a
bookmark.

John Baxter, *A Pound of Paper* (2002).

*****

Most people, especially non-bookish people, are very reluc-
tant to throw away anything that looks like a book. In the most
illiterate houses that one knows every worthless or ephemeral
volume that is bought finds its way to a shelf and stays there. In
reality it is nor merely absurd to keep rubbish merely because it
is printed: it is positively a public duty to destroy it.

J.C. Squire, 'On destroying books' (1927).

Let no book perish, unless it be such an one as it is your
duty to throw into the fire.

Hartley Coleridge, 'William Roscoe' (1833).

The books in this cottage looked particularly disagreeable
– horrid little upstarts of this and that scarlet or cerulean
'series' of 'standard' authors. Having gloomily surveyed them,
I turned my back on them, and watched the rain streaming
down the latticed window, whose panes seemed likely to be
shattered at any moment by the wind. I have known men who
constantly visit the Central Criminal Court, visit also the
scenes where famous crimes were committed, form their own
theories of those crimes, collect souvenirs of those crimes,
and call themselves Criminologists. As for me, my interest in
crime is, alas, merely morbid. I did not know, as those others
would doubtless have known, that the situation in which I
found myself was precisely of the kind most conducive to the

darkest deeds. I did but bemoan it, and think of Lear in the hovel on the heath. The wind howled in the chimney, and the rain had begun to sputter right down it, so that the fire was beginning to hiss in a very sinister manner . . .

I sat down before that blaze. Despair had been warded off. Gloom, however, remained; and gloom grew. I felt that I should prefer any one's thoughts to mine. I rose, I returned to the books. A dozen or so of those which were on the lowest of the three shelves were full-sized, were octavo, looked as though they had been bought to be read. I would exercise my undoubted right to read one of them. Which of them? I gradually decided on a novel by a well-known writer whose works, though I had several times the honour of meeting her, were known to me only by repute.

I knew nothing of them that was not good. The lady's 'output' had not been huge, and it was agreed that her 'level' was high. I had always gathered that the chief characteristic of her work was its great 'vitality.' The book in my hand was a third edition of her latest novel, and at the end of it were numerous press-notices, at which I glanced for confirmation. 'Immense vitality,' yes, said one critic. 'Full,' said another, 'of an intense vitality.' 'A book that will live,' said a third. How on earth did he know that? I was, however, very willing to believe in the vitality of this writer for all present purposes. Vitality was a thing in which she herself, her talk, her glance, her gestures, abounded. She and they had been, I remembered, far too much for me. The first time I met her, she said something that I lightly and mildly disputed. On no future occasion did I stem any opinion of hers. Not that she had been rude. Far from it. She had but in a sisterly, brotherly way, and yet in a way that was filially eager too, asked me to explain my point. I did my best. She was all attention. But I was conscious that my best, under her eye, was not good. She was quick to help me: she said for me just what I had tried to say, and proceeded to show me just why it was wrong. I smiled the gallant smile of a man who regards women as all the more adorable because logic is *not* their strong point, bless them! She asked – not aggressively, but strenuously, as one who dearly loves a joke – what I was smiling at. Altogether a chastening encounter; and my memory of it was tinged with a feeble resentment. How she had scored! . . .

'Has a profound knowledge of human character, and an essentially sane outlook' said one of the critics quoted at the end of the book that I had chosen. The wind and the rain in the chimney had not abated, but the fire was bearing up bravely. So would I. I would read cheerfully and with-out prejudice. I poked the fire and, pushing my chair slightly back, lest the heat should warp the covers, began Chapter I. A woman sat writing in a summer-house at the end of a small garden that overlooked a great valley in Surrey. The description of her was calculated to make her very admirable – a thorough *woman*, not strictly beautiful but likely to be thought beautiful by those who knew her well; not dressed as though she gave much heed to her clothes, but dressed in a fashion that exactly harmonized with her special type. Her pen 'travelled' rapidly across the foolscap, and while it did so she was described in more and more detail. But at length she came to a 'knotty point' in what she was writing. She paused, pushed back the hair from her temples, she looked forth at the valley; and now the landscape was described, but not at all exhaustively, it, for the writer soon overcame her difficulty, and her pen travelled faster than ever, till suddenly there was a cry of 'Mammy!' and in rushed a seven-year-old child, in conjunction with whom she was more than ever admirable; after which the narrative skipped back across eight years, and the woman became a girl, giving as yet no token of future eminence in literature but – I had an impulse which I obeyed almost before I was conscious of it.

Nobody could have been more surprised than I was at what I had done – done so neatly, so quietly and gently. The book stood closed, upright, with its back to me, just as on a book-shelf, behind the bars of the grate. There it was. And it gave forth, as the flames crept up the blue cloth sides of it, a pleasant though acrid smell. My astonishment had passed, giving place to an exquisite satisfaction. How pottering and fumbling a thing was even the best kind of written criticism! I understood the contempt felt by the man of action for the man of words. But what pleased me most was that at last, actually, I, at my age, I of all people, had committed a crime – was guilty of a crime. I had power to revoke it. I might write to my bookseller for an unburnt copy, and place it on the shelf where this one had stood – this gloriously glowing one. I would do nothing of the sort. What I had done I had done. I would wear forever on my conscience the white rose of theft and the red rose of arson. If hereafter the owner of this cottage happened to miss that volume – let him! If he were fool enough to write me about it, would I share my grand secret with him? No. Gently, with his poker, I prodded that volume further among the coals. The all-but-consuming binding shot further little tongues of bright colour – flamelets of sapphire, amethyst, emerald. Charming! Could even the author herself not admire them? Perhaps. Poor woman! – *I* had scored now, scored so perfectly that I felt myself to be almost a brute while I poked off the loosened black outer pages and led the fire on to pages that were pale brown.

These were quickly devoured. But it seemed to me that whenever I left the fire to forage for itself it made little headway. I pushed the book over on its side. The flames closed on it, but presently, licking their lips, fell back, as though they had had enough. I took the tongs and put the book upright again, and raked it fore and aft. It seemed almost as thick as ever. With poker and tongs I carved it into two, three sections

– the inner pages flashing white as when they were sent to the binders. Strange! Aforetime, a book was burnt now and again in the market-place by the common hangman. Was he, I wondered, paid by the hour? I had always supposed the thing quite easy for him – a bright little, brisk little conflagration, and so home. Perhaps other books were less resistant than this one? I began to feel that the critics were more right than they knew. Here was a book that had indeed an intense vitality, and immense vitality. It was a book that would live – do what one might. I vowed it should not. I subdivided it, spread it, redistributed it. Ever and anon my eye would be caught by some sentence or fragment of a sentence in the midst of a charred page before the flames crept over it. 'lways loathed you, bu', I remember; and 'ning. Tolstoy was right.' Who had always loathed whom? And what, what, had Tolstoy been right about? I had an absurd but genuine desire to know. Too late! Confound the woman! – she was scoring again. I furiously drove her pages into the yawning crimson jaws of the coals. Those jaws had lately been golden. Soon, to my horror, they seemed to be glowing grey. They seemed to be closing – on nothing. Flakes of black paper, full-sized layers of brown paper and white, began to hide them from me altogether. I sprinkled a boxful of wax matches. I resumed the bellows. I lunged with the poker. I held a newspaper over the whole grate. I did all that inspiration could suggest, or skill accomplish. Vainly. The fire went out – darkly, dismally, gradually, quite out.

How had she scored again! But she did not know it. I felt no bitterness against her as I lay back in my chair, inert, listening to the storm that was still raging. I blamed only myself. I had done wrong. The small room became very cold. Whose fault was that but my own? I had done wrong hastily, but had done it and been glad of it.

Max Beerbohm, 'The crime' (1920).

9. 'A HISTORY OF ITS OWN'

Books' lives

When they stand on our shelves books seem static, unchanging, inert things. We have only to open them to realize that they have their own lives, even it is merely as mirrors of ourselves.

Oliver Edwards, 'Repeat performance' (1957).

*****

The conditions of a well-bound book may be tersely enumerated. The binding should unite solidarity and elegance. The book should open easily, and remain open at any page you please. It should never be necessary, in reading, to squeeze back the covers; and no book, however expensively bound, has been properly treated, if it does not open with ease. It is a mistake to send recently printed books to the binder, especially books which contain engravings. The printing ink dries slowly, and, in the process called 'beating', the text is often transferred to the opposite page. M. Rouveyre recommends that one or two years should pass before the binding of a newly printed book. The owner will, of course, implore the binder to spare the margins; and, almost equally of course, the binder, *durus arator*, will cut them down with his abominable plough. One is almost tempted to say that margins should always be left untouched, for if once the binder begins to clip he is unable to resist the seductive joy, and cuts the paper to the quick, even into the printed matter . . . Margins make a book worth perhaps

£400, while their absence reduces the same volume to the box marked 'all these at fourpence.'

Andrew Lang, *The Library* (1881).

It is good to fondle a pretty binding, and it is delightful to take down a well-dressed book and caress it, but it would be very like a profanation actually to read it.

Adrian H. Joline, *The Diversions of a Book-Lover* (1903).

And now I am excusing the books geometry, give me leave to excuse its unexpected bulk, and thicknesse, from meer mistake that my writing had not been so close. But I write not this, nor the Book, to any curious in the shapes and outsides of books, or that think it necessary to a Books handsomnesse, (as well as womans) to be slender in the waste; but it is now past cure, and must venture abroad with its faults, materiall, or in printing; which may be more then should, by reason of my distance from the Presse.

Richard Whitlock, *Zootomia* (1654).

The mass of books are like the mass of people; at a distance it is hard to tell them apart. But now and again there is a book which, by the peculiarity of its size, maybe its colour, the individuality of the lettering on its spine, even the way its binding has faded, can be identified at a distance, no matter in what surroundings you come across it.

Oliver Edwards, 'Borrow's letters' (1957).

Indeed, volumes are in their varied external conditions very like human beings. There are some stout and others frail – some healthy and others sickly; and it happens often that the least robust are the most precious. The full fresh health of some of the folio fathers and schoolmen, ranged side by side in solemn state on the oaken shelves of some venerable repository, is apt to surprise those who expect mouldy decay; the stiff hard binding is as angular as ever, – there is no abrasion of the leaves, not a single dog-ear or spot, or even a dust-border on the mellowed white of the margin. So, too, of those quarto civilians and canonists of Leyden and Amsterdam, with their smooth white vellum coats, bearing so generic a resemblance to Dutch cheeses, that they might be supposed to represent the experiments of some Gouda dairymen on the quadrature of the circle.

John Hill Burton, *The Book Hunter* (1863).

In all candour I must say that she approached closely to a realization of the ideals of a book – a sixteenmo, if you please, fair to look upon, of clear, clean type, well ordered and well edited, amply margined, neatly bound.

Eugene Field, *The Love Affairs of a Bibliomaniac* (1896).

*****

There are people who think that the contents of a book are all that really matter – that the questions of type, paper, binding, are merely artistic considerations. This is a great blunder, as every true lover of books knows. The best books will often not give their real message in unsuitable get-up and format. They can never be quite dumb, for intelligence must speak at times or perish. But they are like people – they show to best advantage when they are dressed in well-fitting, suitable clothes.

Anonymous, *Shaded Lights on Men and Books* (1922).

By paying five shillings I have become a member of the Lewes public library. It is an amusing place – full of old ghosts; books half way to decomposition. A general brownness covers them. They are as much alike outwardly as charity schoolchildren. Most have shed their boards years ago, and have been recovered in brown paper.

Virginia Woolf, diary entry 21st September 1919.

I don't recall reading *The Wind in the Willows* as a child, or indeed any of the classics of children's literature. This was partly the library's fault. In those days Armley Junior Library at the bottom of Wesley Road in Leeds bound all its volumes in heavy maroon or black, so that *The Adventures of Milly Molly Mandy* were every bit as forbidding as *The Anatomy of Melancholy*.

Alan Bennett, *The Wind in the Willows: A Play* (1991).

I have had them done up in *Russia*, which will, at any rate, help to give your Library the fine Odour which all Libraries should breathe, as I think.

Edward Fitzgerald, letter to W.A. Wright, 17th November 1869.

Limited edition of 25 copies printed on steam-rolled pig's liver and bound with Irish thongs in desiccated goat-hide quilting, a book to treasure for all time but to lock away in hot weather.

Flann O'Brien, *The Best of Myles* (n.d.).

Kress's had also its version of the Series Books, called, exactly like another series, 'The Camp Fire Girls,' beginning with *The Camp Fire Girls in the Woods*.

I believe they were ten cents each and I had a dollar. But they weren't all that easy to buy, because the series stuck, and to buy some of it was like breaking into a loaf of French bread. Then after you got home, each single book was as hard to open as a box stuck in its varnish, and when it gave way it popped like a firecracker. The covers once prized apart would never close; those books once open stayed open and lay on their backs helplessly fluttering their leaves like a turned-over June bug. They were as light as a matchbox. They were printed on yellowed paper with corners that crumbled, if you pinched on them too hard, like old graham crackers, and they smelled like attic trunks, caramelized glue, their own confinement with one another and, over all, the Kress's smell – bandannas, peanuts and sandalwood from the incense counter. Even without reading them I loved them.

Eudora Welty, 'A sweet devouring' (1947).

I do not believe that the best books like to be included in series of the same size, type, format, and price, as a hundred or a thousand others. They do not like it, any more than an aristocrat would like to be compelled to dine at a shilling table d'hôte. The food might be good enough, but the uniformity would offend him.

Anonymous, *Shaded Lights on Men and Books* (1922).

*****

An old novel has a history of its own. When fresh and new, and before it had breathed its secret, it lay on my lady's table. She killed the weary day with it, and when night came it was placed beneath her pillow. At the seaside a couple of foolish heads have bent over it, hands have touched and tingled, and it has heard vows and protestations as passionate as any its pages contained. Coming down in the world, Cinderella in the kitchen has blubbered over it by the light of a surreptitious candle, conceiving herself the while the magnificent Georgiana, and the Lord Mordaunt, Georgiana's lover, the pot-boy round the corner. Tied up with many a dingy brother, the auctioneer

knocks the bundle down to the bidder of a few pence, and
it finds its way to the quiet cove of some village library,
where with some difficulty – as if from want of teeth – and
with numerous interruptions – as if from lack of memory –
it tells its old stories, and wakes tears, and blushes, and the
laughter as of yore.

Alexander Smith, 'Dreamthorp' (1863).

When a bookmark tumbles out of an old book pristine
and unwrinkled, it is like a gasp of breath from another
century.

Don Borchert, *Library Confidential* (2007).

Papers that have fluttered out of my books as I dust: a
Buenos Aires tramway ticket (trams stopped running in
the late sixties); a phone number and a name I can't place;
a line, *'laudant illa sed ista legunt'*; a bookmark from the
now defunct Librairie Maspéro in Paris; a ticket stub for
Grease; a stub for an Athens–Toronto flight; a bill for
books from Thorpe's in Guildford, still in shillings and
pence; a sticker from Mitchell's Bookstore in Buenos Aires;
a drawing of two ducks or two doves done in red crayon; a
Spanish playing card, the ten of clubs; the address of Estela
Ocampo in Barcelona; a receipt from a store in Milan for
a hat that I don't remember ever owning; a passport photo
of Severo Sarduy; a brochure from the Huntingdon Library
in Pasadena; an envelope addressed to me on George Street
in Toronto.

Alberto Manguel, *A Reading Diary* (2004).

But your own books belong to you; you treat them with
that affectionate intimacy that annihilates formality. Books
are for use, not for show; you should own no book that you
are afraid to mark up, or afraid to place on the table, wide

open and face down. A good reason for marking favourite passages in books is that this practice enables you to remember more easily the significant sayings, to refer to them quickly, and then in later years, it is like visiting a forest where you once blazed a trail. You have the pleasure of going over the old ground, and recalling both the intellectual scenery and your own earlier self.

William Lyon Phelps, 'On books' (1933).

The leaves of the romances, reduced to a condition very like curl-paper, are thickly studded with notes in pencil: sometimes complimentary, sometimes jocose. Some of these commentators, like commentators in a more extensive way, quarrel with one another. One young gentleman who sarcastically writes 'Oh!!!' after every sentimental passage, is pursued through his literary career by another, who writes, 'Insulting beast!' Miss Julia Mills has read the whole collection of these books. She has left marginal notes on the pages, as 'Is not this truly touching? J.M.' 'How thrilling! J.M.' 'Entranced here by the Magician's potent spell. J.M.'

Charles Dickens, 'Our English watering-place' (1858).

Lately, in looking over a copy of Montaigne, I found that some ingenious rebel sympathizer had complacently underscored, with comments, certain passages, which, to him seemed to justify his course. But the sympathizer was followed, on the same page and in the opposite margin, by a fierce loyal pencil, unsparing in epithet, and bitterly sarcastic on the first commentator. Nevertheless, I could not help smiling to think how the old egotistical Michael would have been astonished to have found himself, after three centuries of rest, occupying his old position in a civil war, as wordy at least as any that ever disturbed his conservatism in the flesh. For my own part, whenever I come upon any-thing of this kind that does not please me, I do not seek to answer or refute, but providing myself with a piece if India-rubber I calmly rub out the offensive commentary, and thus consign the critic to oblivion.

Bret Harte, 'Among the books' (1865).

Dear Southey – I have at last been so fortunate as to pick up Wither's Emblems for you, that 'old book and quaint,' as the brief author of *Rosamund Gray* hath it; it is in the most detestable state of preservation, and the cuts are of a fainter impression than I have seen. Some child, the curse of antiquaries and bane of bibliopical rarities, hath been dabbling in some of them with its paint and dirty fingers; and in particular hath a little sullied the author's own por-traiture, which I think valuable.

Charles Lamb, letter to Robert Southey, 18th October 1798.

Another book I browsed a great deal was Malory's *Morte d'Arthur*. I have a copy I remember taking with me when nine years old on a voyage to Madeira, and I am always affected on seeing one of the dirtiest little thumb-marks on that book that I have ever seen on any book.

Stanley Baldwin, 'Books' (1927).

Months ago I bought myself a secondhand copy of Eve Garnett's sweet, strong, deceptively simple *The Family from One End Street* because my original paperback is now 173 separate pages, and I am still racked with guilt at the thought that I have deprived some child from stumbling across its joys in the shop's dusty back room.

Lucy Mangan, 'Remembrance of children's books past' (2007).

This particular book was one of the last of the two thousand to be printed, and sat for longer than the rest in a warehouse in the outskirts of Santiago, absorbing the humidity. From there it was finally sent to a bookstore in Buenos Aires. The careless owner hardly noticed it, and for some years it languished on the shelves, acquiring a pattern of mildew across the cover. It was a slim volume, and its position on the shelf wasn't exactly prime: crowded on the left by an overweight biography of a minor actress, and on the right by the once-bestselling novel of an author that everyone had since forgotten, it hardly left its spine visible to even the most rigorous browser. When the store changed owners it fell victim to a massive clearance, and was trucked off to another warehouse, foul, dingy and crawling with daddy longlegs, where it remained in the dark and damp before finally being sent to a small second-hand bookstore.

Nicole Krauss, *The History of Love* (2005).

Sold last copy of *In Utmost Krutchestan*, at last. It's a pity someone doesn't tell these publishers how difficult it is to sell the last six copies of a book. When you've got a stack of them and they look fresh, they go quite easily. Then the last one sticks. After you've dusted it every week for two or three years you begin to wish the author had never left home.

Brian Aldiss, *The Brightfount Diaries* (1955).

Next to the paper wrappers or jackets, it is the presence of remainders that is the ruin of the modern second-hand book-shop; books more or less written to be remainders, as certain articles, notably field-glasses and opera-glasses, are made to be sold by pawnbrokers.

E.V. Lucas, *Reading, Writing and Remembering* (1932).

There is one interesting consequence of being no mighty big-game hunter. (First folios, black letter, and all the rest of that esoteric paraphernalia are beyond me in more ways than one; I want books only to read.) It is the books in the highways and the byways, the sixpenny boxes, and the barrows that one does meet again and again. Unregarded, unwanted, their ubiquity heightens their distress. What success they must have had in another age to be still so plentiful. What care and enthusiasm was once lavished on them. The attractiveness of their get-up adds to their come-down.

Oliver Edwards, 'Mock laurel' (1957).

Books, no less than their authors, are liable to get ragged, and to experience that neglect and contempt which generally follows the outward and visible sign of poverty. We do therefore most heartily commend the man, who bestows on a battered and shivering volume, such decent and comely apparel, as may protect it from the insults of the vulgar and the more cutting slights of the fair.

Hartley Coleridge, 'William Roscoe' (1833).

If I were a rich man I should found a hospital for homeless aristocratic books . . . I should name it the Home for Genteel Volumes in Decayed Circumstances.

Eugene Field, *The Love Affairs of a Bibliomaniac* (1896).

These were the books on their shelves, old, crumbling: *The Christian's Secret of a Happy Life*. And dusty, brown: *Christ is All*, H.C.G. Moule, London, 1892. Slime-trailed, musty: F.R. Havergal, 1880: *Kept for the Master's Use*. Earwiggy, fading: *Hymns of Faith and Hope*. And *A Basket of Fragments*, R.M. McCheyne, published Aberdeen, no date, pages uncut.

Hilary Mantel, *A Change of Climate* (1994).

Strange indeed are the vicissitudes which befall books, stranger even than the happenings in human life.

Eugene Field, *The Love Affairs of a Bibliomaniac* (1896).

* * * * *

Our books change when they have been borrowed, like our friends when they have been married.

Andrew Lang, *The Library* (1881).

There is nothing so friendly-looking as a well-worn book.

Oliver Edwards, 'Eminently Victorian' (1957).

My old books are Me. I am just as old and thumb-worn as they are.

Anatole France, *The Crime of Sylvestre Bonnard* (1881).

10. 'IT WAS AMAZING REALLY WHERE THE WORD LIBRARIAN WOULD GET YOU'

How little of the din of this stupid world enters into a library.

George Dawson, 'Inaugural address, on the opening of the Birmingham Free Reference Library' (1866).

The habits and manners of certain visitors have fallen more or less under my observations. While I look with distrust on that man, who, having a home, prefers deliberately to sit down to the perusal of a novel or romance in a public library, I am by no means of the opinion that he should be tortured, by unnecessary violence and interruption, to forego his right. But I do not think that the opinion which some visitors entertain – that the appropriate mien for the occasion is a deportment, in which the solemnity of the church-goer and the pitying concern of the hospital visitor are blended – can be said to be properly based. It will be noticed that excessively careful people, in their anxiety to preserve silence, invariably drop a large quarto on the floor, and precipitate a whole shelf in ruins in their frantic efforts to save it. These people usually involve themselves in difficulties with the ladder, ascending that instrument at perilous angles, which bring them presently to grief and lamentation. There is the man who repeats the titles of books audibly, as he walks beside the shelves; the three young ladies who giggle quite as audibly, and who evidently have intentions ulterior to the mere choice of reading matter; the two or three young men, observant of the preceding party yet apparently engaged in studious employment; the man who is hunting authorities, and who is sternly scornful of everybody else and their business; the confidential young lady who requests the librarian to recommend some nice book; the pale theologian, personally aggrieved that Bishop Simkins' admirable pamphlet on Transubstantiation is not found in the catalogue, and the stern moralist who objects that several infidel works *are* to be found therein; the envious man, who longs for the book another has just taken out, and the generous man, who drops in to find himself charged for an interminable array of volumes, taken out by his friends, and himself estopped of his privileges; these are among the individual peculiarities of the library. Add to this the feeling, shared, I think, by all human kind, that the absence of any book we particularly want is a kind of personal affront to our selves – that the librarian and directors are in some way privy to the fact and responsible for it – and you have the general psychological aspect of this, and, indeed, all circulating libraries.

Bret Harte, 'Among the books' (1865).

* * * * *

The Porter spends his days in the Library keeping strict vigil over this catacomb of books, passing along between the shelves and yet never paying heed to the almost audible susurrus of desire – the desire every book has to be taken down and read, to live, to come into being in somebody's mind. He even hands the volumes over the counter, seeks them out in their proper places or returns them there without once realizing that a Book is a Person and not a Thing. It makes me shudder to think of Lamb's *Essays* being carted about as if they were fardels.

W.N.P. Barbellion, diary entry 3rd October 1908.

It was amazing really where the word librarian would get you. As a cover it was perfect: no one suspected librarians of anything, except chronic timidity, and dandruff, and the collecting and issuing of books. Saying to someone you were a librarian was pretty much the equivalent of saying to them, 'No, really, I'm no one, tell me about yourself.' 'Librarian' was the perfect disguise.

Ian Sansom, *The Mobile Library: Mr Dixon Disappears* (2006).

It was a queer enough place. Its only daily point of vitality was at a small table in the centre of the room where reposed a dozen or so of the more recent books. For the town subscribers to the library this was the only interesting spot in the room, for the lady librarian also. She was a dark, heavy, pale-faced woman whose shadow will for ever hover, I fancy, around the memory of all the marvellous books that I read at that time. I am perhaps to-day the human being in all the world who has the most vivid picture of her. She played a fine game at that table, a game of allotting and depriving, a snobbish game, I fear, of keeping the best books for the best people. She would sit upon a choice new volume rather than deliver it over into the hands of someone socially unworthy of it.

Hugh Walpole, *These Diversions: Reading* (1926)

All that summer I used to put on a second petticoat (our librarian wouldn't let you past the front door if she could see through you), ride my bicycle up the hill and 'through the Capitol' (shortcut) to the library with my two read books in the basket (two was the limit you could take out when you were a child and also as long as you lived), and tiptoe in ('Silence') and exchange them for two more in two minutes. Selection was no object. I coasted the two new books home, jumped out of my petticoat, read (I suppose I ate and bathed and answered questions put to me), then in all hope put my petticoat back on and rode those two books back to the library to get my next two.

The librarian was the lady in town who wanted to be it. She called me by my full name and said, 'Does your mother know where you are? You know good and well the fixed rule of this library: *Nobody is going to come running back here with any book on the same day they took it out.* Get both those things out of here and don't come back till tomorrow. And I can practically see through you.'

Eudora Welty, 'A sweet devouring' (1947).

The Library was part of the Institute. Behind a counter was an old man with an ink-pad and a large oval stamp, with which he conducted a passionate, erratic campaign against slack morals. His censorship was quite personal. Some books he could not read and they remained on the shelves in original bindings and without the necessary stigma 'For adults only'. *Roderick Random* stood thus neglected, and *Tristram Shandy*, vaguely supposed to be children's books. *Jane Eyre*, bound and rebound, full of loose leaves, black with grease, fish-smelling, was stamped back and front. *Madame Bovary* had fallen to pieces.

The Librarian who performed this useful service to readers had certain fixed standards before him, as he sat there skimming through the pages, one hand fingering the rubber stamp. Murder he allowed; but not fornication. Childbirth (especially if the character died of it), but not pregnancy. Love might be supposed to be consummated as long as no one had any pleasure out of it. There were single words whose appearance called for the stamp at once. 'Oh, God!' the characters might cry in their extremity, but not 'Oh, Christ!' 'Breast' was not to be in the plural. 'Rape' sent the stamp plunging and twisting into the purple ink.

Elizabeth Taylor, *A View of the Harbour* (1947).

To British Museum after early lunch, arriving about 2 p.m. The first time I have used the Reading Room. A bit awe-inspiring. I felt rather as I mounted the portico that I was entering the abode of death and might be discovered some years later by despairing friends. Some of the attendants in uniform seem dead already and awfully peevish about it.

Maggie Joy Blunt, diary entry 16th April 1947.

From then on, every afternoon, as soon as her mother had left for the bingo, Matilda would toddle down to the library. The walk took only ten minutes and this allowed her two glorious hours sitting quietly by herself in a cosy corner devouring one book after another. When she had read every single children's book in the place, she started wandering round in search of something else.

Mrs Phelps, who had been watching her with fascination for the past few weeks, now got up from her desk and went over to her. 'Can I help you, Matilda?' she asked.

'I'm wondering what to read next,' Matilda said. 'I've finished all the children's books.'

'You mean you've looked at the pictures?'

'Yes, but I've read the books as well.'

Mrs Phelps looked down at Matilda from her great height and Matilda looked right back up at her.

'I thought some were very poor,' Matilda said, 'but others were lovely. I liked *The Secret Garden* best of all. It was full of mystery. The mystery of the room behind the closed door and the mystery of the garden behind the big wall.'

Mrs Phelps was stunned. 'Exactly how old are you, Matilda?' she asked.

'Four years and three months,' Matilda said.

Mrs Phelps was more stunned than ever, but she had the sense not to show it. 'What sort of a book would you like to read next?' she asked.

Matilda said, 'I would like a really good one that grown-ups read. A famous one. I don't know any names.'

Mrs Phelps looked along the shelves, taking her time. She didn't quite know what to bring out. How, she asked herself, does one choose a famous grown-up book for a four-year-old girl? Her first thought was to pick a young teenager's romance of the kind that is written for fifteen year-old schoolgirls, but for some reason she found herself instinctively walking past that particular shelf.

'Try this,' she said at last. 'It's very famous and very good. If it's too long for you, just let me know and I'll find something shorter and a bit easier.'

'*Great Expectations*,' Matilda read, 'by Charles Dickens. I'd love to try it.'

I must be mad, Mrs Phelps told herself, but to Matilda she said, 'Of course you may try it.'

Over the next few afternoons Mrs Phelps could hardly take her eyes from the small girl sitting for hour after hour in the big armchair at the far end of the room with the book on her lap. It was necessary to rest it on the lap because it was too heavy for her to hold up, which meant she had to sit leaning forward in order to read. And a strange sight it was, this tiny dark-haired person sitting there with her feet nowhere near touching the floor, totally absorbed in the wonderful adventures of Pip and old Miss Havisham and her cobwebbed house and by the spell of magic that Dickens the great story-teller had woven with his words. The only movement from the reader was the lifting of the hand every now and then to turn over a page, and Mrs Phelps always felt sad when the time came for her to cross the floor and say, 'It's ten to five, Matilda.'

Roald Dahl, *Matilda* (1988).

If someone came into the mobile, for instance a borrower . . . and they asked for a book, Israel would always start out with good intentions. He'd say, 'Hello! Welcome!' and try to be as cheery as a mobile librarian might reasonably be expected to be, and he might even ask the person if they knew the title of the book they were after, but invariably the person – let's call them Mrs Onions, for the sake of example – would say 'No,' and Israel might manage to remain patient for a moment or two and he might say, 'OK, fine, do you know the name of the author?' but then of course the person – let's say they're still Mrs Onions – would say, 'Och, no,' and Israel would start to struggle a bit then and the person, Mrs Onions, would usually add, 'But you'd know it when you saw it, because it's got a blue sort of a cover, and my cousin had it out last year I think it was, and it's about this big . . .' at which point Israel would lose interest completely, would be incapable of offering anything but his ill-disguised north London university-educated liberal scorn for someone who didn't know what they wanted and didn't know how to get it. But Rosie, Rosie would take it all in her stride and she'd try to find every blue-coloured book in the van and if they didn't have it in, sure they could get a few blue-coloured books in inter-library loan, it was no problem at all.

Ian Sansom, *The Mobile Library: Mr Dixon Disappears* (2006).

The particular vision this time was a brown-haired lass of a Librarian who took no notice of him – even though he'd haunted the Library every day for a week. Cunningly he'd used two tickets, alternating them, as the rules forbade the exchanging of books on the day of borrowing. Thus he was able to come both morning and afternoon.

She wore her hair full and it flowed in a passionate torrent down her back. Her legs were long and lovely, and they made an amorous geometry with Travel and Topography as she sauntered, bosom high among Returned Books to bestow them on the shelves. Once she dropped the books with a noise like thunder.

He rushed to her assistance, but was forestalled by as spotty schoolboy who called her 'Miss' and sniggered with embarrassment when she thanked him with a ravishing smile. Afterwards he contrived to drop an Atlas on the schoolboy's foot, and wondered aloud what children were doing in the grown-up Library.

He made a point of borrowing books in two or more volumes – just so she should linger longer over the stamping while he ogled her fierily, to the disapproval of her more staid colleague.

On the sixth day he determined to speak to her; he intended to ask her out. Desperately he haunted the shelves, clutching three volumes of *The Golden Bough*, till she should be alone at the desk. At last the time came when her colleague was off on a quest in search of Romance for a garrulous old lady. He approached the desk and laid his books upon it.

'What are you doing –?' he began softly, and hesitated slightly between 'this evening' and 'tonight'. But before he could finish, she looked up and said coldly,

'Stamping your books, of course. What do you think? Playing tennis?'

The stamp came down three times, and it was as if his heart had been remorselessly dated for return.

Leon Garfield, *The Book Lovers* (1976).

The most eminent type of this class of men was Magliabecchi, librarian of the Grand-Duke of Tuscany, who could direct you to any book in any part of the world, with the precision with which the metropolitan policeman directs you to St Paul's or Piccadilly. It is of him that the stories are told of answers to inquiries after books, in these terms: 'There is but one copy of that book in the world. It is in the Grand Seignior's library at Constantinople, and is the seventh book in the second shelf on the right hand as you go in.'

John Hill Burton, *The Book Hunter* (1863).

*****

I hope it will not be long before royal or national libraries will be founded in every considerable city, with a royal series of books in them; the same series in every one of them, chosen books, the best in every kind, prepared for that national series in the most perfect way possible; their text printed all on leaves of equal size, broad of margin, and divided into pleasant volumes, light in the hand, beautiful and strong, and thorough as examples of binders' work; and that these great libraries will be accessible to all clean and ordered persons at all times of the day and evening; strict law being enforced for this cleanliness and quietness.

John Ruskin, *Sesame and Lilies* (1864).

Put five books together on a shelf and you have a library. Add another 20,000 volumes and you still have a library – a bigger one, though not necessarily a better one. If all the Library of Alexandria in Egypt had on its shelves when it burned to the ground were Harlequin romances and a few dog-eared Max Brand novels, it would have been a far lesser tragedy. But it was rumoured they had good stuff.

Don Borchert, *Library Confidential* (2007).

Such was my first experience of the addictive excitement a large open-access public library generates: the sense of imminent discovery, the impulse to start on twenty books at once, the decades-old marginal addenda (Surely the problem of free will . . .'), not to mention their several atmospheres: the silence of wet artisan-haunted winter nights, the holiday-fattened shelves of summer afternoons.

Philip Larkin, 'Shelving the issue', *New Statesman* (1977)

The rubber stamp leaves blurred blue numbers on the endpaper. The people choose what is real and what is just a story. Then they carry these things home, free as mushrooms from an autumn hillside, free as blackberries among the broom and wild roses on the banks of a swirling milky river, free as Christmas plums on a wild tree.

Fiona Farrell, *Book Book* (2004).

* * * * *

Another legacy of the past is that the lending library is beyond my comprehension. Even from a friend I would not borrow a book, for fear of what might happen to it in my custody, and also for fear of parting with it when the time comes to give it back. A book, once read, is an acquisition of the spirit, a plant which has struck roots into the soil of the mind; how then can it remain subject to the pettifogging laws of property, like a returned empty? As for borrowing a book from some nameless lender, a book which has been fingered by God knows whom, which is passed round to be enjoyed or desecrated by anyone who pays twopence for the right of handling it, the whole procedure seems to lend itself to only one comparison, which is not elegant.

Arthur Goidel, 'Books' (1946).

I feel uncomfortable having other people's books at home. I want either to steal them or to return them immediately. There is something of the visitor who outstays his welcome in borrowed books. Reading them and knowing that they don't belong to me gives me the feeling of something unfinished, half enjoyed. This is also true of library books.

Alberto Manguel, *A Reading Diary* (2004).

We enjoy reading books that belong to us much more than if they are borrowed. A borrowed book is like a guest in the house; it must be treated with punctiliousness, with a certain considerate formality. You must see that it sustains no damage; it must not suffer while under your roof. You cannot leave it carelessly, you cannot mark it, you cannot turn down the pages, you cannot use it familiarly. And then, some day, although this is seldom done, you really ought to return it.

William Lyon Phelps, 'On books' (1933).

11. 'AN EARLY TASTE FOR READING'

There is perhaps nothing that has a greater tendency to decide favourably or unfavourably respecting a man's future intellect, than the question whether or not he be impressed with an early taste for reading.

> William Godwin, 'Of an early taste for reading' (1797).

One holiday, when she was four, I was so desperate to finish Donna Tartt's *The Secret History* that I took to reading her chunks out loud. Though of course she didn't understand them, she was fascinated. She turned into such a precocious reader herself that on another holiday all three of us were able to sit in a row for hours reading. All those traditional images of holiday nirvana – windsurfing, skiing, moonlight discos: why don't they ever show three people in a row reading?

> Anne Karpf, 'My four-year-old loved reading
> Donna Tartt', *The Guardian*, 5th August 2006.

When Shenstone was a child, he used to have a new book brought to him from the next country-town, whenever any body went to market. If he had gone to bed and was asleep, it was put behind his pillow; and if had been forgotten, and he was awake, his mother (more kindly than wisely) 'wrapped up a piece of wood of the same form, and pacified him for the night'.

> Leigh Hunt, *A Book for A Corner* (1851).

The book was lacking its front cover, the back held on by strips of pasted paper, now turned golden, in several layers, and the pages stained, flecked, and tattered around the edges; its garish illustrations had come unattached but were preserved, laid in. I had the feeling even in my heedless childhood that his was the only book my father as a little boy had had of his own. He had held on to it, and might have gone to sleep on its coverless face: he had lost his mother when he was seven. My father had never made any mention to his own children of the book, but he had brought it along with him from Ohio to our house and shelved it in our bookcase.

Eudora Welty, 'Listening' (1983).

We had our own attic at the top of the house. It was approached by a steep staircase just outside the nursery door. On the left, when you reached the top, were two bedrooms, partitioned off and occupied by the maids. But the rest of the space under the roof was free. One side was used for storing apples, and their musty sweetness pervaded the whole room. There were several chests and wardrobes, full of old wedding-dresses, and many other things which I do not distinctly remember. But here also was the only considerable store of books in the house, a miscellaneous collection of foxed volumes of sermons and devotional works which can have had little appeal to me, but which I pored over with an instinctive love. But two larger tomes were an inexhaustible mine of delight. They were bound volumes of the *Illustrated London News* for the year of the Great Exhibition (presumably 1850), full of the steel engravings of the period.

My lust for books was not satisfied in the attic; I soon craved for novelty. But I must have realized thus early that such a longing was a personal affair, to be fulfilled only by a personal effort. Looking round for a means to this end, I seized on the postman as the only link with the printed world. He came daily on his long pedestrian round, or if there were no letters to bring there was always the *Yorkshire Post*. I made friends with him, and confided to him my secret desires. He was sympathetic, but his acquaintance with literature was limited. It was limited, in fact, to a lurid pink periodical called, I think, *The Police Gazette*, and this he passed on to me; but though I remember the act of reading it, it left no particular impression on me. Evidently its contents had none of the reality of a fairy world.

Herbert Read, *The Innocent Eye* (1933).

Through the open top of its shade, the lamp cast its beams upon a wall entirely corrugated by the backs of books, all bound. The opposite wall was yellow, the dirty yellow of the paper-backed volumes, read, re-read and in tatters. A few 'Translated from the English' – price, one franc twenty-five – gave a scarlet note to the lowest shelf.

Half-way up, Musset, Voltaire, and the Gospels gleamed in their leaf-brown sheepskin. Littré, Larousse, and Becquerel displayed bulging backs like black tortoises, while D'Orbigny, pulled to pieces by the irreverent adoration of four children, scattered its pages blazoned with dahlias, parrots, pink-fringed jellyfish, and duck-billed platypi.

Camille Flammarion, in gold-starred blue, contained the yellow planets, the chalk-white frozen craters of the moon, and Saturn rolling within its orbit like an iridescent pearl.

Two solid earth-coloured partitions held together Élisée Reclus, Voltaire in marbled boards, Balzac in black, and Shakespeare in olive-green.

After all these years, I have only to shut my eyes to see once more those walls faced with books. In those days I could find them in the dark. I never took a lamp when I went at night to choose one, it was enough to feel my way, as though on the keyboard of a piano, along the shelves. Lost, stolen or strayed, I could catalogue them today. Almost every one of them had been there before my birth.

Colette, *My Mother's House* (1922).

Of all the rooms in the house, the Little Bookroom was yielded up to books as an untended garden is left to its flowers and weeds. There was no selection or sense of order here. In dining-room, study, and nursery there was choice and arrangement; but the Little Bookroom gathered to itself a motley crew of strays and vagabonds, outcasts from the ordered shelves below, the overflow of parcels bought wholesale by my father in the sales-rooms. Much trash, and more treasure. Riff-raff and gentlefolk and noblemen. A lottery, a lucky dip for a child who had never been forbidden to handle anything between covers. That dusty bookroom, whose windows were never opened, through whose panes the summer sun struck a dingy shaft where gold specks danced and shimmered, opened magic casements for me through which I looked out on other worlds and times than those I lived in: worlds filled with poetry and prose and fact and fantasy. There were old plays and histories, and old romances; superstitions, legends, and what are called the Curiosities of Literature. There was a book called *Florentine Nights* that fascinated me; and another called *The Tales of Hoffman* that frightened me; and one called *The Amber Witch* that was not in the least like the witches I was used to in the fairy-tales I loved.

Crammed with all sorts of reading, the narrow shelves rose half-way up the walls; their tops piled with untidy layers that almost touched the ceiling. The heaps on the floor had to be climbed over, columns of books flanked the window, toppling at a touch. You tugged at a promising binding, and left a new surge of literature underfoot; and you dropped the book that had attracted you for something that came to the surface in the upheaval. Here, in the Little Bookroom, I learned, like Charles Lamb, to read anything that can be called a book.

Eleanor Farjeon, *The Little Bookroom* (1955).

* * * * *

In common with many only children, especially where the mother is of a grave and home-loving nature, I learned to read at a very early age. Before I was three years old my father would perch me on the breakfast-table to exhibit my one accomplishment to some admiring guest, who admired all the more, because, a small puny child, looking far younger that I really was, nicely dressed, as only children generally are, and gifted with an affluence of curls, I might have passed for the twin sister of my own great doll. On the table I was perched to read some Foxite newspaper, 'Courier' or 'Morning Chronicle', the Whiggish oracles of the day, and as my delight in the high-seasoned politics of sixty years ago was naturally less than that of my hearers, this display of precious acquirements was commonly rewarded, not by cakes or sugar-plums, too plentiful in my case to be greatly cared for, but by a sort of payment in kind. I read leading articles to please the company; and my dear mother recited 'Children in the Wood' to please me. This was my reward; and I looked for my favourite ballad after every performance, just as the piping bullfinch that hung in the window looked for his lump of sugar after going through 'God save the King.' The two cases were exactly parallel.

Mary Russell Mitford, *Recollections of a Literary Life; or, Books, Places, and People* (1851).

She went to the blackboard and printed the alphabet in enormous square capitals, turned to the class and asked,

'Does anybody know what these are?'

Everybody did; most of the first grade had failed it last year. I suppose she chose me because she knew my name; as I read the alphabet a faint line appeared between her eyebrows, and after making me read most of *My First Reader* and the stock-market quotations from *The Mobile Register* aloud, she discovered that I was literate and looked at me with more than faint distaste. Miss Caroline told me to tell my father not to teach me any more, it would interfere with my reading.

'Teach me?' I said in surprise. 'He hasn't taught me anything Miss Caroline. Atticus ain't got time to teach me anything.' I added, when Miss Caroline smiled and shook her head. 'Why, he's so tired at night he just sits in the living room and reads.'

'If he didn't teach you, who did?' Miss Caroline asked good-naturedly. 'Somebody did. You weren't born reading *The Mobile Register.*'

'Jem says I was. He read in a book where I was a Bullfinch instead of a Finch. Jem says my name's really Jean Louise Bullfinch, that I got swapped when I was born and I'm really a – '

Miss Caroline apparently thought I was lying. 'Let's not let our imaginations run away with us dear,' she said. 'Now you tell your father not to teach you any more. It's best to begin reading with a fresh mind. You tell him I'll take over from here and try to undo the damage – '

Harper Lee, *To Kill a Mockingbird* (1960).

Mrs Meiers had a Reading Club on the bulletin board, a sheet of brown wrapping paper with a border of book jackets, our names written in her plump firm hand and after each name a gold star for each book read, but she has given it up because some names have so many stars. Her good readers are voracious and read their weight in books every week, while the slow readers lag behind. Daryl Tollerud has read two books. Mary Mueller has read sixty-seven, and her stars are jammed in tight behind her name. In the encyclopaedia,

I'm up to Customs of Many Lands and she is up to Volcanoes. She is the queen of Reading Club and she knows it.

Garrison Keillor, *Lake Wobegon Days* (1985).

If anyone had to wheel Minelda after school it would have to be Marcia. Marcia did not mind this chore very much, since it let her out of the playing games with the schoolchildren, and besides she felt there was no use arguing about it. She got a book out of the library every day and read as she wheeled. If Minelda yelled too loudly, she was sometimes exasperated to the point of giving her a good pinch. Minelda was two and a half, sickly, and inclined to whimpering, brought on by the thorough manner she was bundled up by her devoted mother, even in summer. Minelda tossed and squirmed under her usually wet woollens, suffering from prickly heat, and her pinched little face was white to the point of blueness. Her steady squirming and tugging at her little harness did not penetrate Marcia's consciousness, absorbed as she was in her book. Even when Minelda managed to wriggle half out of her go-cart, her little caretaker paid no attention, since her sobs presently subsided into chokes as she hung herself by the strap. Sometimes a book would be so entrancing that Marcia, resting the open book on the buggy's handlebar, would be wheeling for several minutes peacefully before noticing that the go-cart was empty.

Dawn Powell, *My Home is Far Away* (1944).

*****

To make boys learn to read and then place no good books within their reach is to give men an appetite and leave nothing in the pantry save unwholesome and poisonous food which depend upon it they will eat rather than starve.

Walter Scott, diary entry 6th December 1825.

A boy's day, in that prepermissive society, was rigidly divided into school, homework (supervised), private tuition for slightly stupid urchins (I was one), a daily walk with Mother for sickly children (I was one), breakfast, supper, dinner and, finally, one hour of reading before bedtime in which to devour my *Tarzans* or my *Captain Nemos*. But they could be read only in short peeks: I had to hide them under volumes of some mandatory Czech classic deemed suitable for my age, more often than not Božena Němcová, the nineteenth-century Romantic concerning whose marital infidelities rumour went about at school, punishable, if somebody told on you, in the good, old, pre-Spockian way. In his armchair on the other side of the coffee table, Father was brooding over his erotic novels by M.B. Böhnel (he had no idea I perused them also: they had beautiful titles – *The Immorals*, *Vice*, *Shame*, *Manhood*, *The Rejuvenated Man*, etc. – but invariably proved disappointing, for this was in the lacklustre preexplicit days); Mother was knitting under her lamp also within sight of my book, and so I mostly only dreamt about the Man of the Apes over blurred lines of the flirtatious Victorian lady.

The big time came after lights out! Cuddled in my bed, I covered myself, head inclusive, with a blanket, from under the mattress I fished out an electric torch, and then indulged in the pleasure of reading, reading, reading. Eventually, often after midnight, I fell asleep from very pleasurable exhaustion.

Josef Škvorecký, 'The pleasures of the freedom to read' (1987).

What do we ever get nowadays from reading to equal the excitement and the revelation in those first fourteen years? Of course I should be interested to hear that a new novel by Mr E.M. Forster was going to appear this spring, but I could never compare that mild expectation of civilized pleasure with the missed heartbeat, the appalled glee I felt when

I found on a library shelf a novel by Rider Haggard, Percy Westerman, Captain Brereton, or Stanley Weyman which I had not read before.

Graham Greene, 'The lost childhood' (1951).

On the 18th day of April last I went to see a friend in a neighbouring Crescent, and on the steps of the next house beheld a group . . . A news-boy had stopped in his walk, and was reading aloud the journal which it was his duty to deliver; a pretty orange-girl, with a heap of blazing fruit, rendered more brilliant by one of those great blue papers in which oranges are now artfully wrapped, leant over the railing and listened; and opposite the *nympham discentem* there was a capering and acute-eared young satirist of a crossing-sweeper, who had left his neighbouring professional avocation and chance of profit, in order to listen to the tale of the little news-boy.

The intelligent reader, with his hand following the line as he read it out to his audience, was saying: – 'And – now – Tom – coming up smiling – after his fall – dee – delivered a rattling clinker upon the Benicia Boy's – potato-trap – but was met by a – punisher on the nose – which,' &c &c; or words to that effect. Betty at 52 let me in, while the boy was reading his lecture; and, having been some twenty minutes or so in the house and paid my visit, I took leave.

The little lecturer was still at work on the 51 doorstep, and his audience had scarcely changed their position. Having read every word of the battle myself in the morning, I did not stay to listen further; but if the gentleman who expected his paper at the usual hour that day experienced delay and a little disappointment I shall not be surprised.

William Makepeace Thackeray,
'On some late great victories' (1869).

Peggotty and I were sitting one night by the parlour fire, alone. I had been reading to Peggotty about crocodiles. I must have read very perspicuously, or the poor soul must have been deeply interested, for I remember she had a cloudy impression, after I had done, that they were a sort of vegetable.

Charles Dickens, *David Copperfield* (1850).

There was a boy called Eustace Clarence Scrubb, and he almost deserved it . . . Eustace Clarence liked animals, especially beetles, if they were dead and pinned on a card. He liked books if they were books of information and had pictures of grain elevators or of fat foreign children doing exercises in model schools.

C.S. Lewis, *The Voyage of the Dawn Treader* (1952).

And I have to be dragged, alternately weeping and shaking with rage, from bookshops in which I find abridged versions of *Little Women* for today's children, whom some fool has decided should not be expected to embrace the whole thing, or having a breakdown in the face of reprints of old favourites (hallelujah!) – but in huge type and bound in garish cartoony and metallic colours that strip them of their dignity and intrigue.

Lucy Mangan, 'Remembrance of children's books past' (2007).

Modern books for children are rather horrible things, especially when you see them in the mass.

George Orwell, 'Bookshop memories' (1936).

My father's sister kept an *everything* shop at Crediton, and there I read through all the gilt-cover little books that could be had at that time, and likewise all the uncovered tales of Tom Hickathrift, Jack the Giant-killer, etc., etc., etc., etc. And I used to lie by the wall and *mope*, and my spirits used to come upon me suddenly; and in a flood of them I was accustomed to race up and down the churchyard, and act over all I had been reading, on the docks, the nettles, and the rank grass. At six years old I remember to have read Belasarius, Robinson Crusoe, and Philip Quarles; and then I found the Arabian Nights' Entertainments, one tale of which (the tale of a man who was compelled to seek for a pure virgin) made so deep an impression on me (I had read it in the evening while my mother was mending stockings), that I was haunted by spectres, whenever I was in the dark; and I distinctly remember the anxious and fearful eagerness with which I used to watch the window in which the books lay, and whenever the sun lay upon them, I would seize it, carry it by the wall, and bask and read. My father found out the effect which these books had produced, and burnt them.

Samuel Taylor Coleridge, letter to
Thomas Poole, 9th October 1797.

I was given only children's books, and they were chosen for me with the greatest care; they were based on the same moral standards as those observed by my parents and teachers; the good were rewarded, and the wicked punished; misadventures befell only those who were vain, ridiculous, and stupid. I accepted the fact that these essential principles were safeguarded for my benefit; usually I did not try to find any relationship between reality and the fantasies I read in books; they amused me, but as it were at a distance, as I would be amused by a Punch and Judy show; that is why, despite the strange ulterior significance that adults ingeniously discover in them, the novels of Madame de Ségur never caused me the slightest astonishment. Madame Bonbec, General Dourakine, together with Monsieur Cryptogame, the Baron de Crac and Bécassine were only animated puppets. A story was something nice in itself, like a marionette show or a pretty picture; I was aware of the necessity informing these constructions which have a beginning, a development, and an end, and in which words and phrases shine with their own peculiar radiance, like colours in a picture. But occasionally a book would speak to me more or less vaguely about the world around me or about myself: then it would make me wonder, or dream, and sometimes it would shake my convictions. Anderson taught me what melancholy is; in his tales, objects suffer from neglect, are broken and pine away without deserving their unhappy fate; the little mermaid, before she passed into oblivion, was in agony at every step she took, as if she were walking on red-hot cinders, yet she had not done anything wrong: her tortures and her death made me sick at heart. A novel I read at Meyrignac, which was called *The Jungle Explorers*, gave me a nasty shock. The author related his extravagant adventures sufficiently well to make me feel I was actually taking part in them. The hero had a friend called Bob, who was rather stout, a good trencherman and absolutely devoted to his companion in danger; he won my sympathies at once. They were imprisoned in an Indian jail: they discovered a subterranean passage just wide enough to let a man crawl along. Bob went first; suddenly he uttered a terrible scream: he had encountered a python. With loudly beating heart and clammy palms I witnessed the grim tragedy: the serpent devoured good old Bob! This story obsessed me for a long time. The mere idea of being swallowed alive was enough to make my blood run cold; but I should have been less shaken if I had disliked the victim. Bob's frightful death made nonsense of all the rules of life: it was obvious, now, that anything could happen.

Simone de Beauvoir, *Memoirs of a Dutiful Daughter* (1958).

The journals were akin to the one New Zealand book Kate actually owned: a prim little volume in a red cover, which her

Auntie Mary and Uncle Frank had given her one year for Christmas: *Our Nation's Story.* Its pictures – The Signing of the Treaty, Governor Hobson – were faded and grey, as if they had hung too long in a dingy room. Boredom coated every page in a powdery mildew. The minute Kate peeled back the holly-leaf paper and saw it, she knew for an absolute fact that Auntie Mary and Uncle Frank truly disliked her.

Fiona Farrell, *Book Book* (2004).

After dinner, Sughrue put the boy to bed, leaving Whitney and me on the patio. I stirred the Indian fire and we listened to Sughrue's voice reading to the boy. It sounded like Dickens.

'Doesn't sound like Dr Seuss,' I said, quietly, as I cracked two more beers. 'More like *Hard Times.*'

'C.W. thinks that children's books don't prepare children for the real world,' she said, not a hint of judgement in her voice.

James Crumley, *Bordersnakes* (1996).

*****

We read so closely, and loved our books so dearly, in the bright, troubled period of boyhood. Eloquence and thought, character and conversation, were but obstacles to brush aside as we dug blithely after a certain sort of incident, like a pig for truffles. For my part, I liked a story to begin with an old wayside inn where, 'towards the close of the year 17–,' several gentlemen in three-cocked hats were playing bowls. A friend of mine preferred the Malabar coast in a storm, with a ship beating to windward, and a scowling fellow of Herculean proportions striding along the beach; he, to be sure, was a pirate. This was further afield than my home-keeping fancy loved to travel, and designed altogether for a larger canvas than the tales that I affected. Give me a highwayman and I was full to the brim; a Jacobite would do, but the highway-man was my favourite dish. I can still hear that merry clatter of the hoofs along the moonlit land; night and the coming of day are still related in my mind with the doings of John Rann or Jerry Abershaw; and the words 'post-chaise,' the 'great North road,' 'ostler,' and 'nag' still sound in my ears like poetry.

Robert Louis Stevenson, 'A gossip on romance' (1882).

There wasn't an adventure story anywhere that was safe from me. 'Come on,' I would say to Miss Roginski when I was well again. 'Stevenson, you keep saying Stevenson. I've finished Stevenson, who now?' and she would say, 'Well, try Scott and see how you like him,' so I tried old Sir Walter and I liked him well enough to butt through a half-dozen books in December (a lot of that was Christmas vacation when I didn't have to interrupt my reading for anything but now and then a little food). 'Who else, who else?' 'Cooper maybe,' she'd say, so off I went into *The Deerslayer* and all the Leatherstocking stuff, and then on my own one day I stumbled onto Dumas and D'Artagnan and that got me through most of February, those guys. 'You have become, before my very eyes, a novel-holic,' Miss Roginski said. 'Do you realize you are spending more time now reading than you used to spend on games? Do you know that your arithmetic grades are actually getting worse?' I never minded when she knocked me. We were alone in the schoolroom, and I was after her for somebody good to devour. She shook her head. 'You're certainly blooming, Billy. Before my very eyes. I just don't know into what.'

I just stood there and waited for her to tell me to read somebody.

'You're impossible, standing there waiting.' She thought a second. 'All right. Try Hugo. *The Hunchback of Notre Dame.*'

'Hugo,' I said. *'Hunchback*. Thank you,' and I turned, ready to begin my sprint to the library. I heard her words sighed behind me as I moved.

'This can't last. It just can't last.'

But it did.

William Goldman, The Princess Bride (1975).

You are what you read, and for a long while I was Rupert the Bear.

John Furnival, 'I, Rupert Schweik' (1994).

The books one reads in childhood, and perhaps most of all the bad and good bad books, create in one's mind a sort of false map of the world, a series of fabulous countries into which one can retreat at odd moments throughout the rest of life, and which in some cases can even survive a visit to the real country they are supposed to represent.

George Orwell, 'Riding down from Bangor' (1946).

The next morning I found a book store and while the others waited in the car I hurried in to make a purchase: the latest volume, in a boxed de luxe edition, of James Branch Cabell.

I was tremendously excited by this act. It was the first expensive book I had ever bought with my own money. The whole trip to Montana for a moment seemed worthwhile, as I stood in the wide dull main street with the book, wrapped, in my hands. I was in love with Cabell and had written him many letters that I had not had the courage to mail. Why, it would change my grandmother's whole life, I used to tell her, if she would only let herself read a few pages of Cabell or listen to me recite them. Now, as the owner of a limited edition, I felt proudly close to him, far closer than to Bob Berdan or to the girls, who were already honking the horn for

me to get in and join the party. They could never understand
– only Cabell would, I supposed – what finding this book in
this out-of-the-way place meant to me. That was the way it
went, in Cabell; horns honked, alarm clocks shrilled, cocks
crowed, to bring the ardent dreamer back to the drab, mean
routines of middle-class reality.

And yet a strange thing happened when I finally opened
the book, taking it carefully from its waxy paper. I was disappointed. I told myself it was not a very *good* Cabell; perhaps
he had written himself out (I knew about that, of course). But
all the while I suspected that it was not the book, which was
no different from other Cabells; it was me. I had 'out-grown'
Cabell, just as older people said I would.

Mary McCarthy, *Memories of a Catholic Girlhood* (1957).

I was looking over a great number of Lamb's [books], of
which no small number are curious. He throws away, indeed,
all modern books, but retains the trash he liked when a boy.

Henry Crabb Robinson, diary entry 9th May 1829.

The early reader may degenerate into an unproductive
pedant, or a literary idler.

William Godwin, 'Of an early taste for reading' (1797).

12. 'THE BOOKS THAT YOU READ WERE ALL I LOVED YOU FOR'

Except some professed scholars, I have often observed that women in general read much more than men; but, for want of a plan, a method, a fixed object, their reading is of little benefit to themselves, or others.

Edward Gibbon, *The Autobiography of Edward Gibbon* (1796).

A comprehensive course of home study, and a guide to books, fit for the highest education of women, is yet a blank page remaining to be filled.

Frederick Harrison, *The Choice of Books
and Other Literary Pieces* (1896).

But Lord George made a course of reading for her – so much for the two hours after breakfast, so much for the hour before dressing – so much for the evening; and also a table of results to be acquired in three months – in six months – and so much by the close of the first year; and even laid down the sum total of achievements to be produced by a dozen years of such work! Of course she determined to do as he would have her do. The great object of her life was to love him; and, of course, if she really loved him, she would comply with his wishes. She began her daily course of Gibbon, after breakfast, with great zeal. But there was present to her an idea, that if the Gibbon had come from her father, and the instigations to amuse herself from her husband, it would have been better.

Anthony Trollope, *Is He Popenjoy?* (1878).

It seems a curiously contradictory fact that, although Englishwomen are on the whole greater readers than men, they are, as book-collectors or bibliophiles, an almost unknown quantity. In France this is not the case, and several books have been published there on the subject of *les femmes bibliophiles*. An analysis of their book-possessions, however, leads one to the conclusion that with them their sumptuously-bound volumes partake more of the nature of bijouterie than anything else. Many of the earlier of these bibliophiles were unendowed with any keen appreciation for intellectual pursuits, and they collected pretty books just as they would collect pretty articles of feminine decoration.

William Roberts, *The Book Hunter in London* (1895).

Men read either the novels it is possible to respect, or detective stories.

George Orwell, 'Bookshop memories' (1936).

Of course there were books. Every proper preparation had been made for rending the little house pleasant. In the evening she took from her shelf a delicate little volume of poetry, something exquisitely bound, pretty to look at, and sweet to handle, and settled herself down to be happy in her own drawing-room. But she soon looked up from the troubles of Aurora Leigh to see what her husband was doing. He was comfortable in his chair, but was busy with the columns of *The Brothershire Herald*.

'Dear me, George, have you brought that musty old paper up here?'

'Why shouldn't I read the *Herald* here, as well as at Manor Cross?'

'Of yes, if you like it.'

'Of course I want to know what's being done in the county.'

But when next she looked, the county had certainly faded from his mind, for he was fast asleep.

Anthony Trollope, *Is He Popenjoy?* (1878).

*****

When a husband is reading aloud, a wife should sit quietly in her chair, relaxed but attentive. If he has decided to read the Republican platform, an article on elm blight, or a blow-by-blow account of a prize fight, it is not going to be easy, but she should at least pretend to be interested. She should not keep swinging one foot, start to wind her wrist watch, file her fingernails, or clap her hands in an effort to catch a mosquito. The good wife allows the mosquito to bite her when her husband is reading aloud.

She should not break in to correct her husband's pronunciation, or tell him one of his socks is wrong side out. When the husband has finished, the wife should not lunge instantly into some irrelevant subject. It's wiser to exclaim: 'How interesting!' or, at the very least, 'Well, well!' She might even complement him on his diction and his grasp of politics, elm blight or boxing. If he should ask some shrewd question to test her attention, she can cry 'Good heavens!' leap up, and rush out to the kitchen on some urgent fictitious errand. This may fool him, or it may not. I hope, for her sake – and for his – that it does.

James Thurber, 'My own ten rules for a happy marriage' (1953).

MISS FANNY '. . . And so the day passed and evening came, black, mysterious, and ghost-like. The wind moaned unceasingly like a shivering spirit, and the vegetation rustled uneasily as if something weird and terrifying were about to happen. Suddenly out of the darkness there emerged a *Man*.

(*She says the last word tremulously but without looking up. The listeners knit more quickly.*)

The unhappy Camilla was standing lost in reverie when, without pausing to advertise her of his intentions, he took both her hands in his.

(*By this time the knitting had stopped, and all are listening as if mesmerised.*)

Slowly he gathered her in his arms –

(*Miss Susan gives an excited little cry.*)

MISS FANNY And rained hot, burning –'

MISS WILLOUGHBY Sister!

MISS FANNY (*greedily*) 'On eyes, mouth –'

MISS WILLOUGHBY (*sternly*) Stop. Miss Susan, I am indeed surprised you should bring such an amazing, indelicate tale from the library.

MISS SUSAN (*with a slight shudder*) I deeply regret, Miss Willoughby. (*Sees Miss Fanny reading quickly to herself.*) Oh Fanny! If you please, my dear.

(*Takes the book gently from her.*)

MISS WILLOUGHBY I thank you.

(*She knits severely*)

MISS FANNY (*a little rebel*) Miss Susan is looking at the end.

(*Miss Susan closes the book guiltily.*)

J.M. Barrie, Quality Street, Act 1 (1902).

Fenichka looked sideways at Bazarov but said nothing. 'What's this book you have?' she asked after a short pause.

'This? It's about science, a very learned book.'

'And are you still studying? Don't you get tired of it? I should think you must know everything by now.'

'Evidently not. You try reading a few lines.'

'Why, I shouldn't understand a thing. Is it in Russian?' Fenichka asked, picking up the heavily bound book in both hands. 'What an enormous book!'

'Yes, it's in Russian.'

'All the same, I shan't understand anything.'

'I didn't give it to you for you to understand it. I want to look at you while you read. When you read, the tip of your nose twitches so endearingly.'

Fenichka, who was about to spell out in a low voice an article on 'Creosote', burst out laughing and threw the book down.

Ivan Turgenev, *Fathers and Children* (1861).

'Do you want me to read to you?'

'First-rate.'

'I know you like me to read sexy stuff.'

'I thought you liked it too.'

'Isn't it basically the person being read to who derives the benefit and satisfaction? When I read to Old Man Treadwell, it's not because I find those tabloids stimulating.'

'Treadwell's blind, I'm not. I thought you liked to read erotic passages.'

'If it pleases you, then I like to do it.'

'But it has to please you too, Baba. Otherwise how would I feel?'

'It pleases me that you enjoy my reading.'

'I get the feeling that the burden is being shifted back and forth. The burden of being the one who is pleased.'

'I want to read, Jack. Honestly.'

'Are you totally and completely sure? Because if you're not, we absolutely won't.'

Someone turned on the TV set at the end of the hall, and a woman's voice said: 'If it breaks easily into pieces, it's called shale. When wet, it smells like clay.'

We listened to the gently plummeting stream of nighttime traffic.

I said, 'Pick your century. Do you want to read about

Etruscan slave girls, Georgian rakes? I think we have some literature on flagellation brothels. What about the Middle Ages? We have incubi and succubi. Nuns galore.'

'Whatever's best for you.'

'I want you to choose. It's sexier that way.'

'One person chooses, the other reads. Don't we want a balance, a sort of give-and-take? Isn't that what makes it sexy?'

'A tautness, a suspense. First-rate. I will choose.'

'I will read,' she said. 'But I don't want you to choose anything that has men inside women, quote-quote, or men entering women. "I entered her." "He entered me." We're not lobbies or elevators. "I wanted him inside me," as if he could crawl completely in, sign the register, sleep, eat and so forth. Can we agree on that? I don't care what these people do as long as they don't enter or get entered.'

'Agreed.'

'"I entered her and began to thrust."'

'I'm in total agreement,' I said.

'"Enter me, enter me, yes, yes."'

'Silly usage, absolutely.'

'"Insert yourself, Rex. I want you inside me, entering hard, entering deep, yes, now, oh."'

I began to feel an erection stirring. How stupid and out of context. Babette laughed at her own lines. The TV said, 'Until Florida surgeons attached an artificial flipper.'

Don DeLillo, *White Noise* (1985).

* * * * *

It has never been explained to my satisfaction why women, as a class, are the enemies of books and are particularly hostile to bibliomania.

Eugene Field, *The Love Affairs of a Bibliomaniac* (1896).

The ladies who have occasion to pass along the quays – in small numbers, however, for they cross the quays, and do not walk along them – are glad to give a glance at the stalls, and do not distain to touch the books with the tips of their gloved fingers. The stall-keepers do not like them very much. They complain of the way in which they hold the books in one hand, of their opening them badly; of their never putting them back in their places; of their turning over their leaves for a long time before deciding to buy, and if by chance they want one, they try to bargain for it as if it were a lobster or a fowl.

Octave Uzanne, *The Book-Hunter in Paris* (1893).

Not once in a blue moon, sir, does womenfolk buy a book. A penny weekly is what they buy, and before they fix on one they read half a dozen. You take my word for it, sir, it takes a woman half an hour to spend a penny at a bookstall.

William Roberts, *The Book Hunter in London* (1895).

I did a very good trade in books, but I brought the prices down at the end considerably, and autographed favourites were going for 3*s*. or even 2*s*. 6*d*. Habit of women of squealing out in ecstasy over name of a book, and then refusing even to consider the purchase of it. Perhaps they were so startled to find that they recognized a title.

Arnold Bennett, diary entry 8th June 1916.

*****

After a time, so far as I can remember, we drew round the fire and began as usual to praise men – how strong, how noble, how brilliant, how courageous, how beautiful they were – how we envied those who by hook or by crook managed to get attached to one for life – when Poll, who had said nothing, burst into tears. Poll, I must tell you, has always been queer. For one thing her father was a strange man. He left her a fortune in his will, but on condition that she read all the books in the London Library. We comforted her as best we could; but we knew in our hearts how vain it was. For though we like her, Poll is no beauty; leaves her shoe laces untied; and must have been thinking, while we praised men, that not one of them would ever wish to marry her. At last she dried her tears. For some time we could make nothing of what she said. Strange enough it was all in conscience. She told us that, as we knew, she spent most of her time in the London Library, reading. She had begun, she said, with English literature on the top floor; and was steadily working her way down to *The Times* on the bottom. And now half, or perhaps only a quarter, way though a terrible thing had happened. She could read no more. Books were not what we thought them. 'Books,' she cried, rising to her feet and speaking with an intensity of desolation which I shall never forget, 'are for the most part unutterably bad!'

Of course we cried out that Shakespeare wrote books, and Milton and Shelley.

'Oh, yes,' she interrupted us. 'You have been well taught, I can see. But you are not members of the London Library.' Here her sobs broke forth anew. At length, recovering a little, she opened one of the pile of books which she always carried about with her – 'From a Window' or 'In a Garden' or some such names as that it was called, and it was written by a man called Benton or Henson, or something of that kind. She read the first few pages. We listened in silence. 'But that's not a book,' someone said. So she chose another. This time it was history, but I have forgotten the writer's name. Our trepidation increased as she went on. Not a word of it seemed to be true, and the style in which it was written was execrable.

'Poetry! Poetry!' we cried, impatiently. 'Read us poetry!' I cannot describe the desolation which fell upon us as she opened a little volume and mouthed out the verbose, sentimental foolery which it contained.

'It must have been written by a woman,' one of us urged. But no. She told us that it was written by a young man, one of the most famous poets of the day. I leave you to imagine what the shock of the discovery was. Though we all cried and begged her to read no more, she persisted and read us extracts from the Lives of the Lord Chancellors. When she had finished, Jane, the eldest and wisest of us, rose to her feet and said that she for one was not convinced.

'Why,' she asked, 'if men write such rubbish as this, should our mothers have wasted their youth in bringing them into the world?'

We were all silent; and, in the silence, poor Poll could be heard sobbing out, 'Why, why did my father teach me to read?'

Virginia Woolf, 'A society' (1921).

*****

Good-looking women don't bother about books.
William Darling, *The Bankrupt Bookseller* (1931).

Mrs Buchanan talked about Mrs Carlyle, whom she had known at Fort Augustus as Jeannie Welsh. She and her very pretty widowed mother were staying there; a clergyman went to call one morning, and finding Greek and Hebrew books scattered about the parlour, he asked, 'What young student have you here?' Oh, it is only Jeannie Welsh,' was the answer. Another who called reported that the mother would get two husbands before the daughter had one: however, this was a mistake, for news came before long that Jeannie had married, 'just a bookish man like herself'.

Caroline Fox, diary entry 15th September 1847.

She saw the young men who came in large numbers to see her sister; but as a general thing they were afraid of her; they had a belief that some special preparation was required for talking with her. Her reputation of reading a great deal hung about her like the cloudy envelope of a goddess in an epic.

Henry James, *Portrait of a Lady* (1881).

'And how do you like being in Germany, Miss Cayhill? Does it not seem very strange after America?'

Johanna lifted her shortsighted eyes to his face, and looked coolly and disconcertingly at him through her glasses, as if she had just become aware of his presence.

'Strange, why should it?'

'Why, what I mean is, everything must be so different from what you are accustomed to – at least it is from what we are used to in England,' he corrected himself. 'The ways and manners, and the language, and all that sort of thing, you know.'

'Excuse me, I do not know,' she answered in the same tone as before. 'If a person takes the trouble to prepare himself for residence in a foreign country, nothing need seem either strange or surprising. But English people, as is well known, expect to find a replica of England in every country they go to.'

There was a pause, in which James, the pianist, who was a regular visitor, approached to have his cup refilled. All the circle knew, of course, that Johanna was 'doing for a new man'; and it seemed to Maurice that James half closed one eye at him, and gave him a small, sympathetic nudge with his elbow.

So he held to his guns. When James had retired, he began anew, without preamble.

'My friend Dove tells me you are interested in German literature?' he said with a slight upward inflection in his voice.

Johanna did not reply, but she shot a quick glance at him, and colouring perceptibly, began to fidget with the tea-things.

'I've done a little in that line myself,' continued Maurice, as she made no move to answer him. 'In a modest way of course. Just lately I finished reading the *Jungfrau von Orleans*.'

'Is that so?' said Johanna with an emphasis which made him colour also.

'It is very fine, is it not?' he asked less surely, and as she again acted as though he had not spoken, he lost his presence of mind. 'I suppose you know it? You're sure to.'

This time Johanna turned scarlet, as if he had touched her on a sore spot, and answered at once sharply and rudely. 'And I suppose,' she said, and her hands shook a little as they fussed about the tray, 'that you have also read *Maria Stuart* and *Tell*, and a page or two of John Paul. You have perhaps heard of Lessing and Goethe, and you consider Heine the one and only German poet.'

Maurice did not understand what she meant, but she had spoken so loudly and forbiddingly that several eyes were turned on them, making it incumbent on him not to take offence. He emptied his cup, and put it down, and tried to give the matter an airy turn.

'And why not?' he asked pleasantly. 'Is there anything wrong in thinking so? Schiller and Goethe *were* great poets, weren't they? And you will grant that Heine is the only German writer who has had anything approaching a style?'

Johanna's face grew stony. 'I have no intention of granting anything,' she said. 'Like all English people – it flatters your national vanity, I presume – you think that German literature began and ended with Heine. – A miserable Jew!'

'Yes, but I say, one can hardly make him responsible for being a Jew, can you? What has that got to do with it?' exclaimed Maurice, this being a point of view that had never presented itself to him. And as Johanna only murmured something that was inaudible, he added lamely: 'Then you don't think much of Heine?'

But she declined to be drawn into discussion, even into an expression of opinion, and the young man continued, with apology in his tone: 'It may be bad taste on my part, of course. But one hears it said on every side. If you could tell me what I ought to read . . . or, perhaps, advise me a little?' he ended tentatively.

'I don't lend my books,' said Johanna more rudely than she had yet spoken. And that was all Maurice could get from her. A minute or two later she rose and went out of the room . . .

Johanna sat alone in her bedroom, at the back of the house. It was a dull room, looking onto a courtyard, but she was always glad to escape to it from the flippant chatter from her sitting room. Drawing a little table to the window, she sat down and began to read. But, on this day, her thoughts wandered; and, ultimately, propping her chin on her hand, she fell into reverie, which began with something like 'the fool and his Schiller!' and ended with her rising, and going to the well-stocked book-shelves that stood at the foot of the bed.

She took out a couple of volumes and looked through them, then returned them to their places on the shelf. No, she said to herself, why should she? What she had told the young man was true: she never lent her books; he would soil them, or worse still, not appreciate them as he ought – she could not give anyone who visited there on Sunday, credit for a nice taste.

Unknown to herself, however, something worked in her, for, the very next time Maurice was there, she met him in the passage, as he was leaving, and impulsively thrust a paper parcel into his hand.

'There is a book, if you care to take it.'

He did not express the surprise he felt, nor did he look

at the title. But Ephie, who was accompanying him to the door, made a face of laughing stupefaction behind her sister's back, and went out on the landing with him to whisper, 'What *have* you being doing to Joan?' – at which remark, and at Maurice's blank face, she laughed so immoderately that she was forced to go down the stairs with him, for fear Joan should hear her.

Henry Handel Richardson, *Maurice Guest* (1908).

He carries a book of poetry around with him in his pocket, sometimes Hölderlin, sometimes Rilke, sometimes Vallejo. In the trains he ostentatiously brings forth his book and absorbs himself in it. It is a test. Only an exceptional girl will appreciate what he is reading and recognize in him an exceptional spirit too. But none of the girls on the trains pay him any attention.

J.M. Coetzee, *Youth* (2002).

I never should have said
The books that you read
Were all I loved you for.

Harriet Wheeler and David Gavurin,
'Here's where the story ends' (1996).

*****

What, after all, is more seductive than the prospect of sinning in libraries?

Michael Dirda, *An Open Book: Chapters
from a Reader's Life* (2003).

She met him next morning in the library. He appeared without warning round the corner of the 821s.

There is the muted sound of people talking at their desks beyond the shelves, the whispery stillness of book row upon row, all their words hushed between covers; there is a smell of old paper, and old glue and a whiff of chip fat from the Student Union cafeteria next door. He walks towards her and when he sees her he makes a little ducking movement with his head as if he might slip sideways down the long aisle between the eighteenth and the nineteenth centuries. But he decides against it almost immediately and continues towards her instead and she for her part walks toward him and they say 'Hi!' as they pass. She does not drop her books in charming confusion, nor does she regard him with eyes heavy with wonder and celandines in her hair as his gaze penetrates to the very soul of her being. But there is a kind of quivering in the air after he has passed, like dust motes jittering in the sunlight through the high windows by the 821s.

Fiona Farrell, *Book Book* (2004).

Love stories are scarce in the library, and this might have something to do with the fact that we tell people to knock it off and take it outside, which is not a good way for a love story to begin. There are quite a few romantics punching the clock for the library, so in the abstract we are rooting for young lovers, but only in the abstract. We don't want urgent fumblings in the adult nonfiction stacks, unzipped jeans, or indiscreet wetness. The janitors will have to bring out their most powerful chemicals and an assortment of disinfectants, and the sharp zip of ammonia will give us all headaches.

Don Borchert, *Library Confidential* (2007).

They'd arrived at the library's IN section – Rhona Carlyle and yon right wee horror Sneery Clearie, her with the waxy eyelids and smell of dog's bum on'r breath.

Clay dumped the Biggles book, then with all the

nonchalance of a one-legged ostrich, he strolled across to the non-fiction area. His heart, a scunnersomely stupid bag of tricks, having decided that he was playing for Scotland and was about to burst the net with a twenty-yarder, turned on all of its taps full bung.

The girls spotted him – it would have been hard not to've seen the watchman's brazier glowing so brightly there in the corner. As they approached, Clay grabbed at a bulky book which, because of its unexpected weight, immediately slipped through his sweaty fingers. It plunged to the floor with a bang that might've been heard as far away as Tradeston, and surely must startle 'Foxy' from his lair. The red-haired fiend seemed to believe that the ears of boys had been provided for him to steer with, rather than for them to hear with: Clay's right appendage began to throb as if in anticipation of the caretaker's pincering grip. Clay saw himself being tugged along in an abject crouching manner, gathering speed as they approached the fateful PUSH-ONLY door through which, having surrendered your library ticket – the hangman's tribute – you were dispatched to the limbo of a bookless universe.

As he bent to lift the book, his nose that'd warned him in a dream that one day it was going to commit suicide without waiting for the rest of his cowardly bits, began to drip. From his trouser pocket – how tight it'd become – he tugged a chunk of floral curtain rag, an action that dragged with it a cascade of jorries; they sped from him in all directions, lodging under tables, below chairs, in darkish corners, even his 'Wizard's Eye', that uncrackable green demon, had fled, but he resisted the urge to pursue it.

Surely now Foxy could come. Clay imagined the caretaker's forbidding door being suddenly whipped open to reveal the terrifying man who'd obviously been disturbed at his dinner for a gore-freckled napkin was loosely tied about his neck and he clutched in his hand the remains of a child's leg

. . . Foxy, however, did not appear; it must be his day off.

The girls drew yet nearer.

Frantically, Clay riffled through his mental phrase-book, trying to pluck from it some passable remark. The weather? Was it still raining? No, it was foggy. When the moment came he stuttered out something totally idiotic: 'Hullo, is it still f-fogging?'

'Still f-fogging what?' asked Sneery Cleerie.

Rhona Carlyle's pale hand rose to glide through the sleek plum darkness of her hair then she turned her head away, probably to hide a grin.

'What's the book?' Sneery now asked.

'Just a book.'

'An awfy big book.'

'Aye.'

'What's it aboot?'

'Things,' said Clay desperately.

'Let's see, then.' Sneery wrested the book from his grasp then began to flap through its pages. 'Aye,' she nodded as she showed one of the book's illustrations to Rhona Carlyle, 'things awright – UNDER-things!'

It turned out that the book was *A History of the Female Costume Through the Ages*!

'You thinking of taking up dressmaking, Tommy?' asked Sneery.

Jeff Torrington, Swing Hammer Swing! (1992).

✳✳✳✳✳

What the old French officer had delivered upon travelling, bringing Polonius's advice to his son upon the same subject into my head – and that bringing in *Hamlet*; and *Hamlet*, the rest of Shakespeare's works, I stopp'd at the Quai de Conti in my return home, to purchase the whole set.

The bookseller said he had not a set in the world –
Comment! said I: taking one up out of a set which lay upon
the counter betwixt us. – He said, they were sent him only
to be got bound, and were to be sent back to Versailles in the
morning, to the Count de B****.

– And does the Count de B****, said I, read Shakespeare?
C'est un Esprit fort, replied the bookseller. – He loves
English books; and what is more to his honour, Monsieur,
he loves the English too. You speak this so civilly, said I, that
'tis enough to oblige an Englishman to lay out a Louis d'or
or two at your shop. – the bookseller made a bow, and was
going to say something, when a young decent girl of about
twenty, who by her air and dress seemed to be *fille de chambre*
to some devout woman of fashion, came into the shop
and asked for *Les Egarements du Coeur & de l'Esprit*: the
bookseller gave her the book directly; she pulled out a little
green sattin purse, run round with a ribband of the same
colour, and putting her finger and thumb into it, she took out
the money and paid for it. As I had nothing more to stay me
in the shop, we both walk'd out at the door together.

Laurence Sterne, *A Sentimental Journey
through France and Italy* (1768).

Mysterious beckonings from behind Art case by Peggy
Ellis. Glancing at one or two customers loitering about shop,
I joined her and asked if anyone was pinching anything.

'No, it isn't that,' she said. 'You see the lady up there with
the white gloves on? . . . Bet you a man with dark wavy hair
joins her in a minute.'

Was serving someone else when he appeared, a harassed,
pleasant-looking chap who at first took no notice of the lady
in white gloves. Gradually he worked his way past the cheap
editions, running a finger along a shelf, until he was close
to her. They spoke quietly together for ten minutes, walking

unostentatiously about the shop and then leaving separately without a touch of the hand – only a lightening of the eyes.

We were better able to discuss the matter thoroughly as not only was Mr Brightfount away on holiday, but Arch Rexine was busy arguing about new shelves with the carpenter in the Slaughterhouse. Dave thought the pair were crooks operating on a grand scale and secretly observing our movts. before pinching every book in the shop. Scorn from Mrs Callow, who said obviously they were lovers. I agreed: they had met by the poetry section.

'They came in just like that on Saturday,' Peggy said. 'Gazed all round the shelves in an odd sort of way and then went out without saying anything.'

The episode quite brightened our day; after all, we lead very secluded lives.

Brian Aldiss, *The Brightfount Diaries* (1955).

*****

When I left Lake Wobegon, Donna Bunsen and I promised each other we'd read the same books that summer as a token of our love, which we sealed with a kiss in the basement. She wore white shorts and a blue blouse with white stars. She poured a cup of Clorox bleach in the washing machine, and then we kissed. In books, men and women 'embraced passionately', but I didn't know how much passion to use, so I put my arms around her and held my lips to hers and rubbed her lovely back, under the wings. Our reading list was ten books, five picked by her and five by me, and we made a reading schedule so that, although apart, we would have the same things on our minds at the same time and would think of each other. We each picked the loftiest books we knew of, such as Plato's *Republic*, *War and Peace*, *The Imitation of Christ*, the *Bhagavad-Gita*, *The Art of Loving*, to have great thoughts to share all summer as we read, but I didn't get far; my copy of Plato sat in my suitcase, and I fished it out only to feel guilty for letting her down so badly. I write her a letter about love, studded with Plato quotes picked out of Bartlett's, but didn't mail it, it was so shameless and false. She sent me two postcards from the Black Hills, and in the second she asked, 'Do you still love me?' I did, but not evidently enough to read those books and become someone worthy of love, so I didn't reply. Two years later she married a guy who sold steel supermarket shelving, and they moved to San Diego.

Garrison Keillor, *Lake Wobegon Days* (1985).

At the table directly opposite us was a rather attractive young couple. Probably a wedding-trip, for the table is covered with flowers. The young man was reading *Les Caves du Vatican*. This is the first time I have ever happened to meet someone actually reading *me* . . . Occasionally he turned toward me and, when I was not looking at him, I felt him staring at me. Lacretelle kept telling me: 'Go ahead! Tell him who you are. Sign his book for him . . .' In order to do this I should have had to be more certain that he liked the book, in which he remained absorbed even during the meal. But suddenly I saw him take a little knife out of his pocket . . . Lacretelle was seized with uncontrollable laughter on seeing him slash *Les Caves du Vatican*. Was he doing so out of exasperation? For a moment I thought so. But no: carefully he cut the binding threads, took out the first few sheets, and handed a whole part of the book that he had already read to his young wife, who immediately plunged into her reading.

André Gide, diary entry 9th January 1930.

J. accused me of always bagging his books as soon as he had begun to read them. I said: 'It's like fishing. I see you've got a bite. I want your line. I want to pull it in.'

Katherine Mansfield, diary entry 30th January 1921.

Best bonus of the solitary life,
late hours, the stack beside the bed as good
as a new lover any night. But now
there's all the courtesies to do, of bedside lights and sex and sleep and who's the first
to shut up shop. Tonight it's me. Your thrill-
er, *Scorcher*, clearly is. I snuggle in,
conscious that you're close but miles away
(in Florida, to be precise). I lie
and listen as the turn of pages slows
down time. The hush-hush sound your thumb's rub makes
is like the lap of waves that lulls me off,
tucked up in self while you, on night watch, learn
whodunnit, why and when and worlds roll by.

Diana Hendry, 'Reading in bed' (2009).

It was getting involved with a voracious reader that seriously changed my relationship with fiction, and turned reading into one of holidaying's main delights. If opening a shared bank account marks a new stage in a relationship, so too does merging your stash of holiday books. Thinking about them, buying them, and anticipating reading them is almost unbearably delicious.

Anne Karpf, 'My four-year-old loved reading Donna Tartt' (2006).

Just two months into our marriage Toryboy has asked me to agree to something so . . . so wrong, so unnatural, so perverse that I can barely find the words to tell you. He wants us to . . . He thinks we are ready to – hang on, I am already typing lying down, but just let me place the sal volatile within easier reach and I'll be back with you . . . OK, here we go: Toryboy thinks that he and I should merge our books.

I know, I know. Incredible. We were lying in bed one

morning and suddenly – 'You know when we move to the new house?' he said.

'Yes, beloved,' I said fondly, as I kicked his legs back to his side of the bed where they belong.

'I think we should put all our books together in that ex-garage bit that we are going to call, over-optimistically and with due sense of irony in the notable absence of anything in the way of mahogany panelling, second Empire sconces and antique Chesterfield seating, The Library.'

I sat up. I drew the sheet up to my neck and gathered the duvet protectively round me.

'Nay, good sirrah! Thou canst not ask it of me!'

'But why not? Lots of people do it.'

Cod-Elizabethan didn't seem to be working so I switched to primary school-teacher in the hope of better luck. 'Oh, and I suppose if lots of people put their copy of Religion and Public Doctrine Vol II on the fire, you'd do it too, would you?'

'You are not reacting as well as one might have hoped. And you're kicking me hard and quite near my genitals.'

'Sorry,' I paused, trying to marshal my thoughts. 'It's just that – it's different for you. Your books are tools. You use them to get information. They tell you facts, you put those facts into your brain, you put the book back on the shelf and don't look at it again unless a cerebral file gets corrupted and you need to look up again who was the 84th riveter on the HMS Asperger in 1863 . . .'

'Frank P Mallenden, born 1839, died 1871 – a riveting accident.'

'. . . Whereas my books are part of me. For the first 19 years of my life, I didn't go out. All my formative experiences are on those shelves. They are me, I am them. They are the reason I have a vocabulary instead of childhood memories. Glasses instead of an adventurous spirit and heavily stamped passport. Incipent scoliosis instead of a varied sexual history. I did not gut them for knowledge and move on. I absorbed them in their entirety and carry them with me still. We are indistinguishable and indivisible. Sometimes, when no one is looking, I take down favourites and hug them. And we do not want to merge with your cold, hard, brutal strangers full of history and politics and war facts. No, no, no, yuck, yuck, yuck, and, finally, no, no, yuck, yuck, no.

I was properly kicking him in the genitals by this point, so it took a while for him to answer, but he continued to press his case and as the night wore on we had reached a workable solution. He can keep his fiction (three Dr Who novels and a set of Wodehouse) in the same room but in a different bookcase from mine, and after a year, if they seem to be getting on, he can start moving in his architecture books. 'But nothing on modernism,' I warn. 'You know it only makes me and mine cry.' He mutters something under his breath. I assume it is congratulations on my willingness to compromise. I hope all of married life is going to be this easy.

Lucy Mangan, 'Teething troubles' (2009).

13. 'TEMPTED IN SO SUBTLE A SHAPE'

The Bibliomania, or the collecting an enormous heap of books without intelligent curiosity, has, since libraries have existed, infected weak minds, who imagine that they themselves acquire knowledge when they keep it on their shelves.

Isaac Disraeli, *Curiosities of Literature* (1807).

Styll I am besy bokes assemblynge,
For to have plenty it is a pleasaunt thynge
In my conceyt, and to have them ay in honde:
But what they mene I do nat understonde.

Sebastian Brant, 'Ship of fools' (1494).

There used to be a story in my days at Cambridge of a book-collecting Don who was fond of discoursing in public of the various crosses he had to bear. He was lamenting one day in Hall the unwieldy size of his library. 'I really don't know what to do with my books,' he said, and looked round for sympathy. 'Why not read them?' said a sharp and caustic Fellow opposite.

A.C. Benson, 'Books' (1906).

*****

There is a bookcase of pitch pine, which contains six hundred books, with glass doors to prevent your getting at them.

No one does try to get at the books, for the Wylies are not a reading family. They like you to gasp when you see so

– 172 –

much literature gathered together in one prison-house, but they gasp themselves at the thought that there are persons, chiefly clergymen, who, having finished one book, coolly begin another.

J.M. Barrie, *What Every Woman Knows*, Act I (1908).

'I want a set of blue books.'

'I don't keep any,' I replied, 'but I will procure what you want from the Stationery Office. What is the subject?'

'The subject?' the dame echoed, 'the subject doesn't matter. I want them in blue.'

The conversation was not so intelligible as what I have written but, at length, I grasped, with the help of a piece of blue tapestry which my customer had in her hand, that it was books of a certain shade of blue binding that she desired – books to match her carpet and the curtains of her drawing room.

I was fortunate and, when my mind had coped with the initial absurdity of the idea of buying books for the colour of their binding, I found her an easy and a profitable client.

William Darling, *The Bankrupt Bookseller* (1931).

I can still see, on one of the highest shelves of the library, a row of volumes bound in boards, with black linen spines. The firmness of the boards, so smoothly covered in marbled paper, bore witness to my father's manual dexterity. But the titles, handwritten on Gothic lettering, never tempted me, more especially since the black-rimmed labels bore no author's name. I quote from memory: *My Campaigns, The Lessons of '70, The Geodesy of Geodesies, Elegant Algebra, Marshal MacMahon seen by a Fellow-Soldier, From Village to Parliament, Zouave Songs* (in verse) . . . I forget the rest.

When my father died, the library became a bedroom and the books left their shelves.

'Just come and see,' my elder brother called one day. In his silent way, he was moving the books himself, sorting and opening them in search of a smell of damp-stained paper, of that embalmed mildew from which a vanished childhood rises up, or the pressed petal of a tulip still marbled like a tree-agate.

'Just come and see!'

The dozen volumes bound in boards revealed to us their secret, a secret so long disdained by us, accessible though it was. Two hundred, three hundred, one hundred and fifty pages to a volume; beautiful, cream-laid paper, or thick 'foolscap' carefully trimmed, hundreds and hundreds of blank pages.

Colette, *Sido* (1929).

*****

They were discussing books, both glorifying in their profound knowledge and *wide reading.*

'Have you read *Dombey and Son*' – 'Yes' – 'That's Dickens isn't it?' – 'Have you read *Tale of Two Cities* – that's Dickens too isn't it. No – Yes. No – Yes.'

One of them, who appeared to have the vaster knowledge of literature, seemed rather piqued when the other said he had read all these books. He would have loved to have stumped him. 'Yes – I haven't read it for a long time, but it all comes back to me.' 'Yes it all comes back.' 'There's Ainsworth – Old St Paul's.' 'Yes, Yes.' 'I know a good book for you to read – you try and get hold it it ---- by ----.'

I think the enlightened one finally recommended a Conan Doyle. They got down to very exciting novels – one of the sea I think – anyway beyond me. I stole a glance at them from the Van Goghs – one was writing with a pencil in his notebook the other was dictating with a satisfied and helping air.

Elizabeth Smart, diary entry 9th March 1933.

For of those who borrow, some read slow; some mean to read but don't read; and some neither read nor meant to read, but borrow to leave you with an opinion of their sagacity.

Charles Lamb, letter to William Wordsworth, April 1815.

It was rather annoying that the tapes which tied the covers of Pepino's poems had got into a hard knot, which she was quite unable to unravel, for she had meant that Daisy should come up, unheard by her, in her absorption, and find her reading Pepino's lyric called 'Loneliness.' But she could not untie the tapes, and as soon as she heard Daisy's footsteps she became lost in reverie with the book lying shut on her lap, and the famous far-away look in her eyes.

E.F. Benson, *Mapp and Lucia* (1935).

I began now to read under the observation of others, and I began, worst of all, to read things because they were difficult, and to fancy that I understood them when most assuredly I did not . . . I remember that I carried about with me at this time an old copy of Landor's *Gebir*, only because I had understood that it was something that almost nobody had read and that it was only appreciated by the very finest spirits. Yes, I carried it about with me, but at this time did not read a word of it, always intending to, loving to see it there lying on my table like some mysterious orchid, and loving it especially when some one picked it up, examined it and wondered that I could be so wise.

Hugh Walpole, *These Diversions: Reading* (1926).

But a slight potential embarrassment nagged at her heart – she couldn't be sure how her library would look to the outside world. She knew, as we all know, how your collection of books can say terrible things about you. She'd dealt with the publishing world for years, but through the medium of an office. She'd never had the books on her shelves inspected by the cruelly all-seeing, judgemental eyes of the literary crowd.

'I can't bear to think of Ed Victor finding something incredibly naff in there,' she said, eyes widening with alarm. 'Or of Jonathan Coe pulling out a novel, leafing through it and shaking his head with incredulity'. Can you, she asked, have a look at it for me?

So I was signed up to edit her library. I had to re-jig it, alphabeticize it, eliminate the once-trend, excise the cheesy and ill-advised, and bring together all the books that had been lying for years in bedroom, lavabo and kitchen and behind the sofa. My function was like that of Hercules cleaning out the Augean stables, until no trace of Paulo Coelho remained.

I had no qualifications of any kind for being a Home Library Advisor, so I made up the rules on the spot. 'Bella,' I said, 'these pots will have to go. And the alabaster ashtray.' She is one of those people whose bookshelves are broken up, spatially speaking, by objets d'art from holidays in Marrakesh, cacti from New Mexico, miniature paintings from Kyoto and charming glass fish from Murano. 'Bookshelves,' I told her sternly, 'are for books only.'

The dog-eared paperbacks had to go as well. ('This is a mature, middle-class library,' I told her crossly, 'not a student-squat bookshelf made from planks and breezeblocks.') No children's books either. No reference books, which should live handily by your desk. And poetry should have a section to itself. Likewise travel . . . Hey! Inventing the Rules of the Modern Library from scratch like this was a piece of cake!

I got to work, removed every hardback book from her shelves, arrayed them across the carpet and began the winnowing process. Abominations that seemed a good idea in the 1970s (*Jonathan Livingstone Seagull*, *The Happy Hooker*) were consigned to the attic, along with works overtaken by history (*Dancing Into History: The Triumph of Seona*

Dancing), political (*The Soviet Empire in the 21st Century*), or technological (*So You Want To Be a Dirigible Pilot?*). I thought it tactful to remove the books with the titles like *Sex and Ageing*, *Living With Cystitis* and *Men Who Hate Women and the Women Who Love Them*. I quietly removed a study of Hitler's compassionate side by David Irving, and silently slid Bella's husband's copy of *The Big Book of Breasts* under the sofa until after the party. Then I nipped off to a handy bookshop to find some up-to-the-minute volumes.

It took hours, but a thing of beauty emerged. The knick-knacks had gone, the medical and psychological advisory stuff was hidden, the Dan Brown novel ('I just wanted to see what all the fuss was about,' Bella wailed) was in the wheelie-bin with Naomi Campbell's *Swan* and Katie Price's *Crystal*.

Now, a perfectly acceptable culture-vulture's library, from Peter Ackroyd to Banana Yamamoto, gleamed from the shelves. A new biography of Garcia Marquez dominated the middle part, cover turned towards the casual browser, while *Stepping Stones*, the new Faber collection of conversations with Seamus Heaney, lay on Bella's coffee-table with a bookmark at page 397 . . . It was fine. The literary world could scrutinize until they were blue in the face, without finding anything to take the piss out of. 'Thank you,' said Bella, 'you've saved me from mortification. You are a cultural superhero.' It was nothing, I said; all in a day's work for Adjust-Your-Library Man.

> John Walsh, 'When the literati come to party, it's
> time to clean up your bookshelves' (2008).

You are a literary man, you never go out, all you ask is to be left alone with your beloved books. But the Man calls. A desultory conversation starts. The Man is peering and poking about your private apartments. You are interested in a book you read recently, and would like to get other people's opinion on it, innocently enough you ask:

'By the way, have you read *Victorian Doctor*?'

'Never heard of it,' the blight says.

'Most interesting book,' you say. 'All about Oscar Wilde's father, gives a very good picture of Dublin life in those days . . . '

'Oh, *that*?', the bore says, his back turned in a very casual way as he interferes with some personal documents on your desk. 'Ah, yes, I read that. Actually he meant to give the book another name, I hadn't heard it was published under that title. I read it in manuscript as a matter of fact.'

Thus you are vouchsafed a glimpse of the anonymous adviser, critic, confessor and daddy christmas of all literary men.

'Ever read *Warren Peace* by T. Allstoy?' you enquire.

'Ah, yes, I read that thing in the manuscript years ago. Is it published yet?'

Flann O'Brien, *The Best of Myles* (n.d.).

To make amends for his show of exasperation he went up to his wife's room and offered to read to her. She was touched, gratefully accepted the offer, and Mr Hutton, who was particularly fond of his accent, suggested a little light reading in French.

'French? I am so fond of French.' Mrs Hutton spoke of the language of Racine as though it were a dish of green peas.

Mr Hutton ran down to the library and returned with a yellow volume. He began reading. The effort of pronouncing perfectly absorbed his whole attention. But how good his accent was! The fact of its goodness seemed to improve the quality of the novel he was reading.

At the end of fifteen pages an unmistakable sound aroused him. He looked up; Mrs Hutton had gone to sleep.

Aldoux Huxley, 'The Gioconda smile' (1922).

* * * * *

It is unfortunate that we New-Yorkers cannot have such delectable shops as those which we encounter in so many of the London streets. To rove, ramble, and revel in the alcoves and about the shelves of those snug and seductive little store-houses is a delight, although it is likewise a torture to the covetous bibliophile who is obliged to count his assets with care and to reckon how far his modest letter of credit will carry him.

Adrian Joline, *The Diversions of a Book-Lover* (1903).

Never poor fellow was tempted in so subtle a shape by Beelzebub as I am. Some he hath assailed as a roaring lion, for others he baits with wine women or wealth but for me there is a book hung in every bookseller's shop.

Robert Southey, letter to Charles Danvers, 6th November 1800.

We all . . . have our particular gin shop, and Mr Gladstone's is a second-hand bookshop.

James Milne, *Memoirs of a Bookman* (1934).

He goes about teasing his friends with his new mathematics. He even frantically talks of purchasing Manning's Algebra, which shows him far gone; for, to my knowledge, he has not been master of seven shillings a good time. George's pockets and —'s brains are two things in nature which do not abhor a vacuum . . . Now if you could step in, in this trembling sus-pense of his reason, and he should find on Saturday morning, lying for him at the Porter's lodge, Clifford's Inn (his safest address,) Manning's Algebra, with a neat manu-scription in the blank leaf, running thus, 'FROM THE AUTHOR,' it might save his wits, and restore the unhappy Author to those studies of Poetry and Criticism which are at present suspended, to the infinite regret of the whole literary world. N.B. – Dirty backs, smeared leaves, and dogs' ears, will be rather a recommendation than otherwise. N.B. – He must have the book as soon as possible, or nothing can withhold him from madly purchasing the book on tick.

Charles Lamb, letter to Thomas Manning, Autumn of 1800.

'Are there not moments,' he asked William, 'when you would also do shameful things to get your hands on a book you have been seeking for years?'

Umberto Eco, *The Name of the Rose* (1980).

'For that mutilated copy of the *Complaynt of Scotland*, I sat out the drinking of two dozen bottles of strong ale with the late learned proprietor, who, in gratitude, bequeathed it to me by his last will. These little Elzevirs are the memoranda and trophies of many a walk by night and morning through the Cowgate, the Canongate, the Bow, Saint Mary's Wynd – wherever, in fine, there were to be found brokers and trokers, those miscellaneous dealers in things rare and curious. How often have I stood haggling on a half-penny, lest, by a too ready acquiescence in the dealer's first price, he should be led to suspect the value I set upon the article! how I have trembled, lest some passing stranger should chop in between me and the prize, and regarded each poor student of divinity that stopped to turn over the books at the stall, as a rival amateur, or prowling bookseller in disguise! And then, Mr Lovel, the sly satisfaction with which one pays the consideration, and pockets the article, affecting a cold indifference, while the hand is trembling with pleasure! Then to dazzle the eyes of our wealthier and emulous rivals by showing them such a treasure as this – (displaying a little black smoked book about the size of a primer) – to enjoy their surprise and envy, shrouding meanwhile under a veil of mysterious consciousness our own superior knowledge and dexterity – these, my young friend, these are the white moments of life.'

Walter Scott, *The Antiquary* (1816).

'They say,' said Urna, 'that he's cleaned out everything from kettles to cobwebs and put a price tag on it. You know, don't you, that he's selling all them old books his grandfather used to have. He's got them in the barn, higgledy-piggledy where the mice can gnaw on them.'

'Has he,' said Hawkheel.

'I suppose you're going up there to look at them.'

'Well,' said Hawkheel, 'I might.'

The Stong place was high on a bluff, a mile upstream from Hawkheel's trailer as the crow flies. To Hawkheel, every turn of the road was like a bite of the auger into the past. He did not remember his adult journeys up Stong's driveway, but recalled with vivid clarity sitting in the dust-coloured passenger seat of their old Ford while his father drove over a sodden mat of leaves. The car window had been cranked down, and far below, the hissing river, heavy with rain, cracked boulders along its bottom. His father drove jerkily, lips moving in whispered conversation with invisible imps. Hawkheel had kept his hand on the door handle in case the old man steered for the edge and he had to jump. It was one of the last memories he had of his father.

The Stong place, he saw now, had run down. The real-estate agents would get it pretty soon. The sagging clapboard house tapered away into a long ell and the barn. The store was still in the ell, but Harkheel took the old shortcut around back, driving through the singing nettles and just catching a glimpse through the store window of Stong's white head bobbing over handful of papers.

The barn was filled with dim, brown light shot through like Indian silk with brilliant threads of sunlight. There was a faint smell of apples. On the other side of the wall a rooster beat his wings. Hawkheel looked around and saw, behind the grain sacks, hundreds of books, some in boxes, some stacked on shelves and windowsills. The first one he took up was a perfect copy of Thad Norris's 1865 *The American Angler's Book*. He'd seen it listed in his catalogue at home at $85. Stong wanted one dollar.

Hawkheel went at the boxes. He turned out Judge Nutting's nice little book on grouse, *The History of One Day Out of Seventeen Thousand*. A box of stained magazines was hiding a rare 1886 copy of Halford's *Floating Flies*, the slipcase deeply marked with Stong's pencilled price of $1.50.

'Oh god,' said Hawkheel, 'I got him now.'

He disguised the valuable books by mixing them with dull-jacketed works on potatoes and surveying, and carried the stack into the feed store. Stong sat at the counter, working his adding machine. Hawkheel noticed he had taken to wearing overalls, and a bandana knotted around his big neck. He looked to see if there was a straw hat on a nail.

'Good to see you, Leverd,' said Stong in a creamy voice. He gossiped and joked as if Hawkheel was one of the summer people, winked and said, 'Don't spend your whole security check on books, Leverd. Save a little out for a good time.'

E. Annie Proulx, 'On the antler' (1988).

'Do you know something? You Spaniards have a story about a bookseller in Barcelona who committed murder. Well, I'd be capable of killing for a book too.'

I wouldn't recommend it. That's how it all starts. It doesn't seem like a big deal but then you end up lying, voting in elections, things like that.'

'Even selling one's books?'
'Even that.'

Arturo Pérez-Reverte, *The Dumas Club* (1993).

*****

He said that when he had been buying a book too many he would leave it at the club and then take it home last thing at night, after his wife was in bed, and hide it.

Arnold Bennett, diary entry 2nd October 1915.

He buys a lot of books and daren't take them home. I had over twenty collected for him when he called this afternoon with his car and chauffeur. 'My wife has gone to her sister's,' he said, 'I will get my books home today.'

He takes them home and puts them behind other books. He dare not buy more bookshelves, so he double-banks the books he has.

William Darling, *The Bankrupt Bookseller* (1931).

*****

Or poetry readings in the shop, where we drew curtains across the shelves to prevent excessive stealing. Stealing was rife from the professionals. No matter how hard we watched them during the day they always managed to secrete the books, art books particularly, under their coats as they turned and made for the front door. We couldn't challenge them unless we had proof. Occasionally one of us would walk to the door if we suspected a professional at work and stand there in an attempt to discourage them, to let them know we were wise to their activity, the gauntlet thrown down for them to take the risk of being confronted. Many still accomplished their task. Checking the shelves after their departure, one could not believe a book could still be missing despite close scrutiny. The poets were the most incompetent book thieves, or 'borrowers', as one told me some years later. We watched them clumsily sticking books away in a bag, or beneath their jackets. If only they had asked, they would have received a good deal.

Paul Buck, 'Street of dreams' (2006).

In all the books of a certain cunning bibliophile he had the price written in plain figures; when anyone asked him for the loan of a book he invariably replied, 'Yes, with pleasure,' and looking in the volume further added, 'I see the price of this work is £2 17s. 6d.' – or whatever the value happened to be – 'you may take it at this figure, which will, of course, be refunded when the volume is returned.' If a person really wished to read the volume he would of course be glad to leave this deposit; and if he did not return it he would not be altogether an unmitigated thief.

William Roberts, *The Book Hunter in London* (1895).

'I was once in an inn parlour', said another reader recently, 'which had only three books, and one of them was the Poetical Works of Mr Thomas Little, the quite amusing and improper amorous verses with which Moore began his career, and a rare volume. It is no longer in that inn parlour,' he added. (Why are book-lovers so dishonest?)

E.V. Lucas, 'Other people's books' (1909).

* * * * *

Many a poet or artist . . . would spend the day seated on a bench, reading and making notes as if in a regular library, and then appear with a volume and ask if we had a less expensive, shop-soiled copy of the same. For some reason we used to find such a copy on the floor at our feet with a slight mark as if a foot had been placed on it. Not worth its price, now. Sold.

Paul Buck, 'Street of dreams' (2006).

The shop, in a narrow court once favoured by purveyors of *curiosa*, is, naturally, shut: no problem, Howard kicks the lock and the door breaks open. There's no light, that's been cut, but beyond the counter are two unemployable Outpatients defying their limits by the glow of a hurricane lamp.

One of them is working with sandpaper to erase the inhibiting announcement 'damaged stock', from the fore-edges of a pile of bought-in publishers' successes of last month. There's nothing 'damaged' about them, except the stamp: and that is being swiftly remedied. The Outpatient's knees are white with the flakes of falling paper. He coughs.

The second Outpatient is hunched over a kettle steaming the labels out of a collection of oversized fine art library books. If there are easier ways to earn your breakfast, he is incapable of imagining them.

The shelves in the shop, as illuminated by Dryfield's torch in a tunnel of unbelievable light, are rich with the direst dreck, condemned tea-chest gloom, most of the books covered in a layer of tea grains, brown, lumpy, inert. Strictly for the captive student market, yards of instant grant-bleeders.

The gelt is everywhere.

Behind one of the stacks is a roped-off stairway that lets us down into the basement. And here the best of the Outpatients, a man whose abilities almost lift him to the rank of Scuffler, sits beside a candle, two handed, signing, with mantra-like automatism, a stack of newly-minted first editions. Who would have thought that John Fowles needed to moonlight? Or that John Fowles and Dick Francis were one and the same: the left hand and the right hand.

The Ian Fleming presentations have already been taken away, to weather, overnight, under a desk lamp.

Iain Sinclair, *White Chappell, Scarlet Tracings* (1987).

*****

This is the secret which no essayist and no poet has either ever discovered or has ever had sufficient courage to put into print: all the best books belong to other people.

It is more than a secret: it is a tragedy, because do what one will one cannot have the same books as other people. If one were to go to a bookseller and lead him to a friend's house, and say, 'Spare no expense; make me an exact reproduction of this library,' he could not do it. Something would be missing. The next time one visited one's friend again, one would see his latest acquisition, and it would be so desirable that it would take away the flavour of all other books; although as a matter of fact that would have gone already, because they had become one's own and no longer were another's . . .

I do not suggest that one has this covetous feeling in a public library, or in the British Museum Reading Room, or even in a bookshop. One may lack the books one sees there, but one does not covet them. The reason, I think, is that that which one is coveting in a friend's room as one looks at his shelves is not (if one only knew it) so much certain of his books as the temperament that made certain of his books necessary to him. One is for the moment envious of his character. One wants the book because it is his; one almost resents the circumstance that he should have had the wit or the sympathy to acquire that work. The cheek of the man!

E.V. Lucas, 'Other people's books' (1909).

14. 'AN INTENSE GRIEVANCE'

Having nothing to read

There are those to whom the having nothing to read is an intense grievance. They instinctively look round for a book wherever they go, and they are often bitterly disappointed. It is a predicament indeed to be landed on a visit where the house is destitute of books, and where no library is near. I have heard of a reader so insatiable that he tried to get squints into odd volumes even during the penitential process of morning calls. This is a length to which few would go, but I am with the same writer when he says that he would rather read a list of hotels or a week-old advertisement sheet than do without reading at all.

W. Robertson Nicoll, *A Bookman's Letters* (1913).

I'm got into the West, over the Hills and far away. Here is nothing to be lik'd that I can find, every thing in [the] same Mode and fashion as [the] Days of King Arthur and the knights of the round table. In the Hall, a great shovel board Table and antic suite of Armour, the parlor finished with right reverend turky work Chairs and Carpets, and For books, the Famous History of Amadis de Gaul, and the Book of Martyrs, with wooden Cuts, and for companny not a mortal man but the parson of the parish, some fourscore or thereabouts.

Lady Mary Wortley Montague, letter to
Anne Justice, 12th June 1710.

When the opportunity of trial came, [I] set sail with nothing more satisfying than the *Field Service Pocket Book*, which weighs 6½ ounces and is an authorized molecule of the 35 lb to which a subaltern's baggage is well known to be restricted. It is an admirable compendium, closely printed on thin paper; I soon wished for variety. For months I subsisted on newspapers in languages I imperfectly understood, and on a flotsam of novels washed up by the Aegean or purchased of the *librarie française, rue Venezelos*; and was hardly conscious of any craving for better fare till luck bought me the Poet Laureate's *Spirit of Man*. Its candid covers are soiled now to the hue of our tunics, and its leaves probably smell of stables and stale tobacco; but every printed line is precious. If there be still any Gentlemen of England who sit at home in ease, and hop like elderly sparrows from shelf to shelf of their well-appointed libraries, tell them they do not know what a Book can be.

R.W. Chapman, 'Proper names in poetry' (1920).

I learned, firsthand, about the void that all devoted readers dread – the void that yawns just past the last page of whatever good book we're currently reading.

Maureen Corrigan, *Leave Me Alone: I'm Reading* (2005).

*****

Children are so modern, have so much liberty, seem to know so clearly what they want that they read what they please, I suppose. But when I was young, thirty years ago, there were the strongest views about this; certain books only must be read on Sunday and many books, of course, not at all, and it must have been just at this time that an aunt of mine discovered me with a cheap edition of Ouida's *Under Two Flags* and burnt it publicly before the assembled family, afterwards restoring to me very ceremoniously the sixpence that I had spent upon it.

Hugh Walpole, *These Diversions: Reading* (1926).

The existence of public libraries was kept from me as long as possible (the knowledge would, it was thought, interfere with my studies).

Philip Larkin, 'Shelving the issue' (1977).

It was a far cry from the respectable Miss Edgeworth to a series of Beadle's 'Dime Novels'. I looked on them as delectable but inferior. There was a prejudice against them in well-brought-up households; but if you thoughtfully provided yourself with a brown paper cover, which concealed the flaring yellow of Beadle's front page, you were very likely to escape criticism.

Maurice Francis Egan, *Confessions of a Book-Lover* (1923).

They had brought with them a few books, and Widdowson, after breakfast, sat down by the fire to read. Monica first of all wrote a letter to her sister; then, as it was still impossible to go out, she took up one of the volumes that lay on a side-table in their sitting-room, novels left by former lodgers. Her choice was something or other with a yellow back. Widdowson, watching all her movements furtively, became aware of the pictured cover.

'I don't think you'll get much good out of that,' he remarked, after one or two efforts to speak.

'No harm, at all events,' she replied, good-humouredly.

'I'm not so sure. Why should you waste your time? Take "Guy Mannering" if you want a novel.'

'I'll see how I like this first.'

He felt himself powerless, and suffered acutely from the thought that Monica was in rebellion against him.

George Gissing, *The Odd Women* (1893).

One morning I paused before the Catholic fellow's desk.

'I want to ask you a favour,' I whispered to him.

'What is it?'

'I want to read. I can't get books from the library, I wonder if you'd let me use your card?'

He looked at me suspiciously.

'My card is full most of the time,' he said.

'I see,' I said and waited, posing my question silently.

'You're not trying to get me into trouble, are you, boy?' he asked, staring at me.

'Oh, no, sir.'

'What book do you want?'

'A book by H.L. Mencken.'

'Which one?'

'I don't know. Has he written more than one?'

'He has written several.'

'I didn't know that.'

'What makes you want to read Mencken?'

'Oh, I just saw his name in the newspaper,' I said.

'It's good of you to want to read,' he said, 'But you ought to read the right things.'

I said nothing. Would he want to supervise my reading?

'Let me think,' he said. 'I'll figure out something.'

I turned from him and he called me back. He stared at me quizzically. 'Richard, don't mention this to the other white men,' he said.

'I understand,' I said. 'I won't say a word.'

A few days later he called me to him.

'I've got a card in my wife's name,' he said. 'Here's mine.'

'Thank you, sir.'

'Do you think you can manage it?'

'I'll manage fine,' I said.

'If they suspect you, you'll get into trouble,' he said.

'I'll write the same kind of notes to the library that you

wrote when you sent me for the books,' I told him. 'I'll sign your name.'

He laughed.

'Go ahead. Let me see what you get,' he said.

That afternoon I addressed myself to forging a note. Now, what were the names of books written by H.L. Mencken? I did not know any of them. I finally wrote what I thought would be a foolproof note: *Dear Madam, Will you please let this nigger boy* – I used the word 'nigger' to make the librarian feel that I could not possibly be the author of the note – *have some books by H.L. Mencken?* I forged the white man's name.

I entered the library as I had always done when on errands for whites, but I felt that I would somehow slip up and betray myself. I doffed my hat, stood a respectful distance from the desk, looked as unbookish as possible, and waited for the white patrons to be taken care of. When the desk was cleared of people, I still waited. The white librarian looked at me.

'What do you want, boy?'

As though I did not possess the power of speech, I stepped forward and simply handed her the forged note, not parting my lips.

'What books by Mencken does he want?'

'I don't know, ma'am,' I said, avoiding her eyes.

'Who gave you this card?'

'Mr Falk,' I said.

'Where is he?

'He's at work, at the M— Optical Company,' I said. 'I've been in here for him before.'

'I remember,' the woman said. 'But he never wrote notes like this.'

Oh, God, she's suspicious. Perhaps she would not let me have the books? If she had turned her back at that moment, I would have ducked out the door and never gone back. Then I thought of a bold idea.

'You can call him up, ma'am,' I said, my heart pounding.

'You're not using these books, are you?' she asked pointedly.

'Oh no, ma'am. I can't read.'

'I don't know what he wants by Mencken,' she said under her breath.

I knew now that I had won; she was thinking of other things and the race question had gone out of her mind. She went to the shelves. Once or twice she looked over her shoulder at me, as though she was still doubtful. Finally she came forward with two books in her hand.

'I'm sending him two books,' she said. 'But tell Mr Falk to come in next time, or send me the names of the books he wants. I don't know what he wants to read.'

I said nothing. She stamped the card and handed me the books. Not daring to glance at them, I went out of the library.

Richard Wright, *Black Boy: A Record of Child and Youth* (1937).

At two minutes past five one Tuesday afternoon the venerable Bishop of Stortford, entering the room where his daughter Katherine sat, found her engrossed in what he presumed to be a work of devotion but which proved on closer inspection to be a novel entitled *Cocktail Time*. Peeping over her shoulder, he was able to read a paragraph or two. She had got, it should be mentioned, to the middle of Chapter 13. At 5-5 sharp he was wrenching the volume from her grasp, at 5-6 tottering from the room, at 5-10 in his study scrutinizing Chapter 13 to see if he had really seen what he had thought he had seen.

He had.

At 12-15 on the following Sunday he was in the pulpit of the church of St Jude the Resilient, Eaton Square, delivering a sermon on the text 'He that touches pitch shall be defiled' (Ecclesiasticus 13-1) which had the fashionable congregation rolling in the aisles and tearing up the pews. The burden of his address was a denunciation of the novel *Cocktail Time* in the course of which he described it as obscene, immoral, shocking, impure, corrupt, shameless, graceless and depraved, and all over the sacred edifice you could see eager men jotting the name down on their shirt cuffs, scarcely able to wait to add it to their library list.

P.G. Wodehouse, Cocktail Party (1958).

LYDIA Here, my dear Lucy, hide these books – quick, quick – fling *Peregrine Pickle* under the toilet – throw *Roderick Random* into the closet – put *The Innocent Adultery* into *The Whole Duty of Man* – thrust *Lord Aimworth* under the sofa – cram Ovid behind the bolster – there – put *The Man of Feeling* into your pocket – so, so, now lay Mrs Chapone in sight, and leave Fordyce's *Sermons* open on the table.

LUCY O burn it, ma'am, the hairdresser has torn away as far as 'Proper Pride'.

LYDIA Never mind – open at 'Sobriety' – fling me Lord Chesterfield's *Letters*.

Richard Brinsley Sheridan, The Rivals (c.1773).

If, instead of being folios, quartos, octavos, and the like, the Judge's books were buxom, blithe maidens, his wife could hardly be more jealous of the Judge's attentions to them than she is under existing circumstances. On one occasion, having found the Judge on two successive afternoons sitting alone in the library with Pliny in his lap, this spirited lady snatched the insidious volume from her husband's embraces and locked it up in one of the kitchen's pantries; nor did she release the object of her displeasure until the Judge had promised solemnly to be more circumspect in the future, and had further mollified his wife's anger by bringing home a new silk dress and a bonnet of exceptional loveliness.

Eugene Field, *The Love Affairs of a Bibliomaniac* (1896).

* * * * *

Supposing we made book-buying harder instead of easier? Would this not create a demand, human nature being what it is?

Visions attended me in afternoon of a book rationing system that would make the yearly 13,000 new books or whatever it is a scarcity instead of, honestly, a glut. ('I'm afraid this coupon doesn't entitle you to a whole Mee's *Children's Encyclopaedia*, madam; but we can do you a volume of the *Oxford Junior.*' Or, 'No sir, these white ones are only valid for paper-backs. You have to forfeit two of the mauve coupons for a cloth-bound edition.' Or, 'Sorry, we cannot accept Book Tokens until you produce a certificate from your oculist.' Or even, 'The queue on the far side of the shop is for art books, madam; at present you're in the queue for Black Market Bibles.')

Brian Aldiss, *The Brightfount Diaries* (1955)

* * * * *

But how can I live here without my books? I really seem to myself crippled and only half myself.

Balthazar Bonifacius Rhodiginus (1656) quoted in J. Baldwin, *The Book-Lover: A Guide to the Best Reading* (1893).

Dear Miss Dyer – I am very uneasy about a *Book* which I either have lost or left at your house on Thursday. It was the book I went out to fetch from Miss Buffam's, while the tripe was frying. It is called 'Phillip's Theatrum Poetarum' but it is an English book. I think I left it in the parlour. It is Mr Cary's book, and I would not lose it for the world. Pray, if you find it, book it at the Swan, Snow Hill, by an Edmonton stage immediately, directed to Mr Lamb, Church-street, Edmonton, or write to say you cannot find it. I am quite anxious about it. If it is lost, I shall never like tripe again.

Charles Lamb, letter to Mrs Dyer, 22nd December 1834.

He was alone with his books, and had to choose among them, which he should take and save. They numbered several hundred, including a shelf of the very first books he had read to himself. A large proportion consisted of the books of his youth. Having been lived through by the eager, docile Stodham, these poems, romances, essays, autobiographies, had each a genuine personality, however slight the difference of its cover from its neighbour's. Another class represented aspirations, regrets, oblivions: half cut, dustier than the rest, those wore strange, sullen, ironical, or actually hostile looks. Some had been bought because it was inevitable that a young man should have a copy. Others, chiefly volumes in quarto or folio, played something like the part of portraits in a house of one of the new-rich. An unsuspecting ostentation had gone with some affectation to their purchase. They gave a hint of 'the dark backward and abysm of time' to that small room, dingy, but new . . . He leaned against the hot wall, receiving their various looks, returning them. Several times he bent forward to clutch this one or that, but saw another which he could not forsake for it, and so left both. He moved up close to the rows: he stood on tip-toe, he knelt. Some books he touched, others he opened. He put each one back. The room was silent with memory. He might have put them all in safety by this time. The most unexpected claims were made. For example, there was a black-letter 'Morte d'Arthur' in olive

calf. He had paid so much for it that he had to keep its existence secret: brown paper both concealed and protected it. He
did, in fact, put this with a few others, chosen from time to
time, on a chair. Only a very few were without any claims –
histories and the like, of which there are thousands of copies,
all the same. The unread and the never-to-be read volumes
put in claims unexpectedly. No refusal could be made without
a qualm. He looked at the select pile on the chair dissatisfied.
Rather than take them only he would go away empty. 'You
had better look sharp, sir,' said a fireman, vaulting over the
desk. Mr Stodham looked at the mute multitude of books
and saw all in a flash. Nevertheless not one could he make up
his mind to rescue.

Edward Thomas, *The Happy-Go-Lucky Morgans* (1913).

Over coffee one afternoon in the summer of 2001, András
reminded me of another way to burn books, explained to
him by a colleague who survived the siege of Sarajevo. In the
winter, the scholar and his wife ran out of firewood, and so
began to burn their books for heat and cooking. 'This forces
one to think critically,' András remembered his friend saying.
'One must prioritize. First, you burn old college textbooks,
which you haven't read in thirty years. Then there are the
duplicates. But eventually, you're forced to make altogether
tougher choices. Who burns today: Dostoevsky or Proust?' I
asked András if his friend had any books left when the war
was over. 'Oh yes,' he replied, his face lit by a flickering smile.
'He still had many books. Sometimes, he told me, you look at
the books and just choose to go hungry.'

Matthew Battles, *Library: An Unquiet History* (2003).

*****

If I did not feel that my eyes begin to fail me, I should find in the undiminished pleasures of reading an assurance of never-ceasing or declining enjoyment in old age.

Henry Crabb Robinson, diary entry 25th November 1827.

Then, my dear Eyes not having quite recovered the paraffin, a lad comes to read at half-past seven till nine – stumbling at every other word, unless it be some Story that carries him along. So now we are upon the Woman in White.

Edward Fitzgerald, letter to W.F. Pollock, 7th December 1869.

You can read merely to pass the time, or you can read with an overt urgency, but eventually you will read against the clock.

Harold Bloom, *How to Read, and Why* (2000).

INDEX OF AUTHORS

SUBJECT INDEX

REFERENCES AND
COPYRIGHT NOTICES

Aldiss, Brian. (2001 [1955]) *The Brightfount Diaries*, London: House of Stratus. Reproduced with permission of Curtis Brown Group Ltd. London on behalf of Brian Aldiss. Copyright © Brian Aldiss 1955.

Amis, Martin. (1985 [1984]) *Money*, Penguin: Harmondsworth. Published by Jonathan Cape, reprinted by permission of The Random House Group Ltd.

Anderson, W.E.K. (ed.) (1972) *The Journal of Walter Scott*, Clarendon Press: Oxford.

Anonymous (1922) 'Books read on Christmas day' in *Shaded Lights on Men and Books*, Andrew Melrose Ltd: London.

Ascham, Roger (1934 [1571]) *The Scholemaster*, G. Bell and Sons, Ltd: London.

Auden, W.H. (1963) 'The guilty vicarage' in *The Dyer's Hand and Other Essays*, Faber and Faber: London.

Austen, Jane (n.d. [1818]) *Northanger Abbey*, Blackie and Sons: London.

Bailey, Paul (2004) 'Treasure trove' *Guardian*, 20th November.

Baldwin, Stanley (1938) 'Books' in *Our Inheritence*, Hodder and Stoughton: London.

Barbellion, W.N.P. (1948 [1919]) *Journal of a Disappointed Man,* Penguin: Harmondsworth.

Barker, Pat (1996 [1995]) *The Ghost Road*, Penguin, London.

Barrie, J. M. (1896) *Sentimental Tommy: the Story of his Boyhood*, Cassell: London.

Barrie, J. M. (n.d.) *The Plays of J.M. Barrie in One Volume*, Hodder and Stoughton: London.

Battles, Matthew (2003) *Library: An Unquiet History*, William Heinemann: London. Copyright © Matthew Battles. Used by permission of W.W. Norton & Company, Inc.

Baxter, John (2002) *A Pound of Paper: Confessions of a Book Addict*, Doubleday: London.

Baxter, Richard (1678) *A Christian Directory: or, A Summ of Practical Theologie, and Cases of Conscience, Directing Christians how to Use their Knowledge and Faith; How to Improve all Helps and Means, and to Perform all Duties; How to Overcome Temptations and Escape or Mortifie Every Sin*, Robert White: London.

Beecher, H. W. (1882) *Lectures to Young Men on Various Important Subjects*, Wakefield: William Nicholson and Sons.

Beerbohm, Max (1950 [1920]) 'The crime' in *And Even Now*, Wm Heinemann: London.

Bell, A.O. (1977) *The Diary of Virginia Woolf, vol I: 1915–1919*, The Hogarth Press: London.

Benjamin, Walter trans. H. Zohn (1999 [1931]) 'Unpacking my library' in M.W. Jennings, H. Eiland and G. Smith (eds) *Walter Benjamin, Selected Writings vol 2, 1927–34*, Belknap Press of Harvard University: London. Copyright © 1968 by Harcourt Brace Jovanovich, Inc.

Bennett, Alan (1991) *The Wind in the Willows: A Play*, Faber and Faber: London.

Benson, A.C. (1906) 'Books', *From a College Window,* Thomas Nelson and Sons Ltd.: London.

Benson, E.F. (2004 [1935]) *Mapp and Lucia*, Penguin: London.

Birrell, Augustine (1905) 'Book buying', in *In the Name of the Bodleian, and Other Essays*, Elliot Stock: London.

Block, Lawrence (1990 [1979]) *The Burglar who Liked to Quote Kipling*, No Exit Press: Harpenden.

Bloom, Harold (2001 [2000]) *How to Read and Why*, Fourth Estate: London.

Blunt, Maggie Joy, diary entries in S. Garfield (2004) *Our Hidden Lives*, The Ebury Press: London.

Borchert, Don (2007) *Library Confidential*: Virgin Books: London.

Brant, S. trans. R. Pynson [1494] 'Ship of fools', quoted in T. Dibdin (1809) *The Bibliomania; or Book Madness*, Longman, Hurst, Rees and Orme: London.

Breit, H. and Lowry, M.B. (1985) *Selected Letters of Malcolm Lowry*, Penguin: Harmondsworth.

Bronte, C. (1977 [1847]) *Jane Eyre*, Penguin: Harmondsworth.

Browning, Elizabeth Barratt (1882 [1856]) *Aurora Leigh*, Smith, Elder and Co.: London.

Buck, Paul (2006) http://www.visionsofthecity.com/streetofdreams01.htm and also in 'Heart of the matter' in I. Sinclair (ed.) *London: City of Disappearances*, Hamish Hamilton: London. Printed with permission.

Burney, Fanny (1940 [1846]) *The Diary of Fanny Burney*, J.M. Dent and Sons Ltd: London.

Burton, John Hill (1863 [1862]) *The Book Hunter*, William Blackwood and Sons: Edinburgh.

Bury, Richard de trans. E.C. Thomas (1960 [1345]) *Philobiblon*, Basil Blackwell: Oxford.

Butler, Edward (1885) 'A table talk on books and reading' in *For Good Consideration*, Elliot Stock: London.

Campbell, R.T. (1984 [1946]) *Bodies in a Bookshop: A Detective Story*, Dover: New York.

Canetti, Elias (1965 [1935]) *Auto da Fé*, Penguin: Harmondsworth.

Cervantes, M. trans. J.M. Cohen (1981 [1614]) *Don Quixote*, Penguin: Harmondsworth.

Chapman, R.W. (1920) 'The portrait of a scholar' in *Portrait of a Scholar and Other Essays written in Macedonia 1916-18*, Oxford University Press: London.

Coetzee, J.M. (2002) *Youth*, Secker and Warburg: London. Reprinted with permission.

Coleridge, E.H. (ed.) (1895) *Letters of Samuel Taylor Coleridge*, William Heinemann: London.

Coleridge, H. (1833) 'William Roscoe' in *Biographia Borealis, or Lives of Distinguished Northerns*, London: Whitaker, Treacher and Co.

Coleridge, Samuel Taylor (1930 [1817]) *Biographia Literaria*, J.M. Dent and Sons: London.

Coleridge, Samuel Taylor, for *Letters* see Coleridge, E.H.

Colette (1968 [1922]) *My Mother's House* and *Sido*, Penguin: Harmondsworth.

Collier, J. (1985 [1930]) *His Monkey Wife*, Oxford: Oxford University Press. (© John Collier, 1930). Excerpt reproduced by permission of PFD (www.pfd.co.uk) on behalf of The Estate of John Collier.

Collins, W. (2005 [1859]) *The Queen of Hearts*, 1st World Library: Fairfield IA.

Corrigan, M. (2006 [2005]) *Leave Me Alone: I'm Reading*, Vintage Books: New York.

Croft-Cooke, Rupert (1960) *English Cooking: A New Approach*, W.H. Allen: London.

Crumley, James (1998 [1996]) *Bordersnakes*, London: Flamingo.

Currey, K. (1965) *New Letters of Robert Southey*, Columbia University Press: London.

Dahl, Roald (1989 [1988]) *Matilda*, Puffin Books: London. Used by permission of www.penguin.com.

Darling, William (1960 [1931]) *The Bankrupt Bookseller*, Robert Grant and Son Ltd: Edinburgh.

Dawson, G. (1866) 'Inaugural address on the opening of the Birmingham Free Reference Library' in A. Ireland (ed.) (1883) *The Book Lover's Enchiridion: Thoughts on the Solace and Companionship of Books*, Simkin, Marshall and Co.: London.

de Beauvoir, Simone, trans. J. Kirkup (1981 [1958]) *Memoirs of a Dutiful Daughter*, Penguin: Harmondsworth. Copyright © 1958 by Librairie Gallimard. Translation copyright © 1959 by The World Publishing Company.

DeLillo, D. (2002 [1985]) *White Noise*, Picador: London. Copyright © 1984, 1985 by Don DeLillo. Used by permission of Viking Press, a division of Penguin Group (USA) Inc.

Dickens, Charles (1980 [1850]) *David Copperfield*, Harmondsworth: Penguin.

Dickens, Charles (1984 [1843-4]) *Martin Chuzzlewit*, Penguin: Harmondsworth.

Dickens, Charles (n.d. [1858]) 'Our English watering-place' in *Miscellaneous Papers*, Hazell, Watzon and Viney Ltd: London.

Dirda, Michael (2004 [2003]) *An Open Book: Chapters from a Reader's Life*: W. W. Norton, London.

Disraeli, Benjamin, for *Letters* see Zetland, Marquis of.

Disraeli, Isaac (1893 [1807]) *Curiosities of Literature,* George Routledge and Sons Ltd: London.

Doherty, Pete (2006), quoted in the *Guardian*, 3rd October.

Driffield, B.C.M. (1986) *All the Secondhand and Antiquarian Bookshops*, BCM Driffield: London.

Eco, Umberto (1984 [1980] *The Name of the Rose*, Picador: London.

Edwards, Oliver (1957) 'Borrow's letters', 'Eminently Victorian', 'Mock laurel', 'Reading aloud', 'Repeat performance' and 'To kill the Count' in *Talking of Books,* Heinemann: London.

Egan, Maurice Frances (1923) *Confessions of a Book-Lover*, Doubleday, Page and Company: New York.

Elkin, S. (1992) *Pieces of Soap*, Simon and Schuster: New York.

Emerson, Ralph Waldo (1903 [1860]) 'Books' in *The Complete Prose Works of Ralph Waldo Emerson*, Ward, Lock and Co. Ltd: London.

Fadiman, C. (1946) *Reading I've Liked*, Hamish Hamilton: London.

Farjeon, E. (1972 [1955]) *The Little Bookroom*, Oxford University Press: London. Printed with permission.

Farrell, Fiona (2004) *Book Book*, Vintage: Auckland. Printed with permission.

Field, Eugene (1896) *The Love Affairs of a Bibliomaniac*, Charles Scribner's Sons: New York.

Fielding, Henry (1935 [n.d.]) 'On taste in the choice of books' in W. Peacock (ed.) *Selected English Essays*, Oxford University Press: London.

Fitzgerald, Edward, for *Letters* see Wright, W.A.

Forman, M.B. (1960) (ed.) *The Letters of John Keats*, Oxford University Press: London.

Fox, Caroline, for *Letters* see Pym, H.N.

France, Anatole trans. L. Hearn (1908 [1881]) *The Crime of Sylvestre Bonnard*, John Lane: London.

Frost, W.H. (1900) *Fairies and Folk of Ireland*, Charles Scribner's Sons: New York.

Fuller, Roy (1962 [1953]) *The Second Curtain*, Penguin: Harmondsworth.

Garfield, L. (1976) *The Book Lovers*, Ward Lock Limited: London.

Garfield, S. (2004) *Our Hidden Lives*, The Ebury Press: London. Diary entries reproduced with permission of Curtis Brown Group Ltd, London on behalf of the Trustees of the Mass Observation Archive. Copyright © The Trustees of the Mass Observation Archive.

Gettmann, R.A. (1961) *George Gissing and H.G.Wells: Their Friendship and Correspondence*, Rupert Hart-Davis: London.

Gibbon, Edward, for *Autobiography* see Sheffield, Lord.

Gide, André trans. Justin O'Brien (1967 [1949]) *Journals 1889–1949*, Harmondsworth: Penguin. © Editions Gallimard, Paris 1939.

Gissing, G., for *Correspondence* see Gettman, R.A.

Gissing, G. (2000 [1893]) *The Odd Women*, Oxford: Oxford University Press.

Gissing, G. (1961 [1903]) *The Private Papers of Henry Ryecroft*, Harvester Books: Brighton.

Godwin, W. (1797) 'Of an early taste for reading', in *The Enquirer: Reflections on Education, Manners and Literature*, Robert Campbell and Co.: Philadelphia.

Goidel, Arthur (1946) 'Books' in *Alphabet for Odette*, Methuen and Co. Ltd.: London.

Goldman, William (1976 [1975]) *The Princess Bride*, Pan: London.

Gorky, M. trans. S.Koteliansky, 'On literature' [n.d.] in F. H. Pritchard (ed.) (1929) *Great Essays of All Nations*, George G. Harrap and Co. Ltd: London.

Grand, Sarah (1983 [1897]) *The Beth Book*, Virago: London.

Greene, Graham (1966 [1951]) *The Lost Childhood*, Penguin: Harmondsworth. Printed with permission.

Grierson, F. (1911) 'The making of books' and 'The past and present' in *The Humour of the Underman and Other Essays*, Stephen Swift and Co.: London.

Grossmith, G. & W. (1972 [1892]) *The Diary of a Nobody*, Penguin: Harmondsworth.

Grundy, I. (ed.) *Lady Mary Wortley Montatgue: Selected Letters*, Penguin: London.

Hardy, Thomas (1971 [1895]) *Jude the Obscure*, Macmillan: London.

Hare, A.W. & J.C. (1897 [1827]) in P.E.G. Girlestone (ed.) *Guesses at Truth: Selections from the Work of Augustus and Julius Hare*, George Routledge and Sons Ltd: London.

Harrison, Frederick. (1896) *The Choice of Books and Other Literary Pieces,* Macmillan: London.

Harte, Bret, 'Among the books' [1865] in Bret Harte and Mark Twain (1927 [1864–7]) *Sketches of the Sixties*, John Howell: San Francisco.

Hazlitt, William, 'On going a journey' [1821] and 'On the pleasure of hating' [1826] in R. Blythe (ed.) (1985) *Selected Writings*, Penguin: Harmondsworth.

Hendry, Diana (2008) 'Reading in bed' in *Late Love & Other Whodunnits*, York: Peterloo/Mariscat Press. Printed with permission.

Higginson, T.W. (1904) 'Books unread', *Atlantic Monthly*, March.

Hoban, Russell (1974 [1973]) *The Lion of Boaz-Jachin and Jachin-Boaz*, Picador: London.

Hollowood, Bernard (1948) 'Reading time' in *Scowle and Other Papers*, Penguin: West Drayton.

Hornby, Nick (2006) 'Can't put it down?' *Guardian*, 30th September.

Hornby, Nick (2007 [2006]) *The Polysyllabic Spree*, Penguin: London. Copyright © Nick Hornby, 2006.

Hudson, D. (1967) *The Diary of Henry Crabb Robinson: An Abridgement*: Oxford University Press: London.

Hunt, Leigh (1885 [1850]) *Autobiography*, Smith, Elder and Co.: London.

Hunt, Leigh (1851) *A Book for a Corner*, Chapman and Hall: London.

Hunt, Leigh (1876 [1847]) 'Bookstalls and "Galateo"' and 'Jack Abbott's breakfast' in *Men, Women and Books*, Smith, Elder and Co.: London.

Huxley, A. (1944 [1922]) 'The Gioconda smile', *Twice Seven*, The Reprint Society: London. Copyright © 1957 by Mrs Laura Huxley, by permission of Ivan R. Dee, publisher.

Jackson, Holbrook (1950 [1930]) *The Anatomy of Bibliomania*, Faber and Faber: London. Reprinted with permission of The Society of Authors as the literary representative of the Estate of Holbrook Jackson.

James, Henry (1976 [1881]) *The Portrait of a Lady*, Penguin: London.

Joline, Adrian (1903) *The Diversions of a Book-Lover*, Harper and Brothers: New York.

Kafka, Franz trans. R. & C. Wilson (1978) *Letters to Friends, Family and Editors*, John Calder: London.

Karpf, A. (2006) 'My four-year-old loved reading Donna Tartt', *Guardian*, 5th August.

Keats, John, for *Letters* see Forman, M.B.

Keillor, Garrison (1986 [1985]) *Lake Wobegon Days*, Faber and Faber: London. Printed with permission.

Kipling, R. (1912) 'The uses of reading,' in *A Book of Words*, Macmillan and Co.: London.

Koestler, Arthur (1973) *The Call Girls: A Tragi-Comedy*, Random House: New York.

Krauss, Nicole (2006 [2005] *The History of Love*, London: Penguin. Copyright © 2005 *The History of Love* (W.W. Norton) by Nicola Krauss. Reprinted with permission by Melanie Jackson Agency, LLC.

Lamb, C. (n.d.) *The Letters of Charles Lamb*, Simkin, Marshall, Hamilton, Kent and Co.: London.

Lamb, C. (1929 [1823]) 'Old china', in *The Last Essays of Elia*, Oxford University Press: London.

Lang, A. (1902) 'Bibliomania', *Cornhill Magazine*.

Lang, A. (1881) *The Library*, Macmillan and Co.: London.

Larkin, P. (1977) 'Shelving the issue,' *New Statesman*, 10th June.

Latham, R. And Matthews, W. (1976) *The Diary of Samuel Pepys*, London: G. Bell and Sons Ltd.

Lee, Harper (1963 [1960]) *To Kill a Mockingbird*, Penguin: Harmondsworth.

Letts, M. (1942) *The Old House: A Generation of Lawyers*, Frederick Miller: London.

Lewis, C.S. (1978 [1952]) *The Voyage of the Dawn Treader*, Penguin: Harmondsworth. © C.S. Lewis Pte. Ltd. 1952. Extract reprinted with permission.

Lively, Penelope (1985 [1984]) *According to Mark*, Penguin: London.

Lowry, Malcolm, for *Letters* see Breit, H. and Lowry, M. B.

Lucas, E.V. (1936) 'The *guide* supreme' in *Only the Other Day: A Volume of Essays*, Methuen and Co., London.

Lucas, E.V. (1909) 'On reading aloud' and 'Other people's books' in *One Day and Another*, Methuen and Co., London.

Lucas, E.V. (1932) *Reading, Writing and Remembering*, Methuen and Co., London.

Macaulay, Lord, for *Letters* see Trevelyan, G.O.

Macdonald, F. (1911) *Recreations of a Book-Lover*, Hodder and Stoughton: London.

Mangan, Lucy, (2008) '2008 – the year I'm gonna get cultured,' *Guardian*, 29th December. Printed with permission.

Mangan, Lucy (2007) 'I'm alphabetising my books – oh no!' *Guardian*, 10th February. Printed with permission.

Mangan, Lucy (2007) 'Remembrance of children's books past,' *Guardian*, 30th June. Printed with permission.

Mangan, L. (2009) 'Teething troubles', *Guardian*, 17th January. Printed with permission.

Manguel, A. (2004) *A Reading Diary*, Canongate Books: Edinburgh. © Alberto Manguel, c/o Guillermo Schavelzon and Asociados, Agencia Literaria info@schavelzon.com

Mansfield, Katherine, for *Journal* see Murray, J.M.

Mantel, Hilary (1995 [1994]) *A Change of Climate*, Penguin: London.

Mathews, William (1877) *Hours with Men and Books*, Belford Brothers: Toronto.

Maugham, W. Somerset (1948 [1938]) *The Summing Up*, William Heinemann: London.

Maurois, André (1929) 'Advice to a young Frenchman starting for England' in F.H. Pritchard (ed.) *Great Essays of All Nations*, George G. Harrap and Co.: London. Copyright © André Maurois 1929, reproduced by permission of Curtis Brown Ltd., London.

McCarthy, Mary (1965 [1957]) *Memories of a Catholic Girlhood*, Penguin: Harmondsworth. Printed with the permission of the Mary McCarthy Literary Trust.

Meredith, G. (1912 [1876]) *Beauchamp's Career*, The Times Book Club: London.

Milne, James (1934) *Memoirs of a Bookman*, John Murray: London.

Minghella, Anthony (2000) *The Talented Mr Ripley: A Screenplay by Anthony Minghella*, Methuen: London.

Mitford, Mary Russell (1857 [1851]) *Recollections of a Literary Life; or, Books, Places and People*, Richard Bentley: London.

Montague, Lady Mary Wortley, for *Letters* see Grundy, I.

Montaigne, M. de, trans. J.M. Cohen (1973 [1580]) 'On three kinds of relationships' in *Essays*, Penguin: Harmondsworth.

Moore, G. (1936 [1924]) *Conversations in Ebury Street,* William Heinemann Ltd: London.

Morley, Christopher (1940 [1932]) *Human Being*, Random House: United States.

Morrissy, Mary (1993) 'Bookworm' in *A Lazy Eye*, Jonathan Cape: London. Reproduced by permission of Green and Heaton Ltd.

Murray, M. J. (ed.) *Journal of Katherine Mansfield*, London: Constable.

Nicoll, W. R. (1913) *A Bookman's Letters,* Hodder and Stoughton, London.

O'Brien, Flann (1993) 'Book handling' in *The Best of Myles*, Flamingo: London. Copyright © 1968 Flann O'Brien. Reproduced by permission of A. M. Heath and Co., Ltd.

Oliver, Denis (2007) quoted by J. Harris 'Into the void', *Guardian*, 3rd February.

Orwell, George 'Bookshop memories' [1936] and 'Riding down from Bangor' [1946], in (1984) *The Penguin Essays of George Orwell*, Penguin: Harmondsworth. Copyright © 1946 by Sonia Brownell Orwell and renewed 1974 by Sonia Orwell reprinted by permission of Houghton Mifflin Harcourt Publishing Company.

Pain, Barry (2006 [1900–13]) *The Eliza Stories*, Prion Books Ltd: London.

Partridge, Frances (1978) *A Pacifist's War*, Robin Clark: London.

Pepys, Samuel, for *Diary* see Latham, R. and Matthews, W.

Pérez-Reverte, Arturo trans. S. Soto (2003 [1993]) *The Dumas Club*, Vintage: London.

Phelps, William Lyon (1933) 'On books', radio broadcast 6th April transcribed at http://www.wlpf.org/

Powell, Dawn (1999 [1944]) *My Home is Far Away*, Steerforth Press: South Royalton, Vermont.

Proulx, E. Annie (1995 [1988]) 'On the antler' in *Heartsongs*, Simon and Schuster: New York.

Proulx, E. Annie (1994 [1993]) *The Shipping News*, Fourth Estate: London.

Proust, Marcel trans. J. Sturrock (1988 [1905]) 'Days of reading (1)' in *Against Sainte-Beuve and Other Essays*, Penguin: London.

Pym, H. N. (1882) *Memories of Old Friends, being Extracts from the Journals and Letters of Caroline Fox*, London: Smith, Elder and Co.

Quiller-Couch, A. (1896 [1894]) 'The attitude of the public towards letters' and 'The poor little Penny Dreadful' in *Adventures in Criticism*, Cambridge University Press: Cambridge.

Read, Herbert (1933) *The Innocent Eye*, Faber and Faber Ltd: London.

Rhodiginus, Balthazar Bonifacius, quoted in J. Baldwin (1893) *The Book-Lover: A Guide to the Best Reading*: G. P. Putnam and Sons: London.

Richardson, Henry Handel (n.d. [1908]) *Maurice Guest*, McLean, VA: IndyPublish. Published with permission of The Estate of Henry Handel Richardson.

Richardson, Henry Handel (1964 [1948]) *Myself When Young*, William Heinemann Ltd: London.

Roberts, Michèle (1993 [1987]) *The Book of Mrs Noah*, Minerva: London.

Roberts, William (1895) *The Book Hunter in London. Historical and Other Studies of Collectors and Collecting*, E. Stock: London.

Robinson, Henry Crabb, for *Diary* see Hudson, D.

Roosevelt, Theodore (1916) *A Book Lover's Holiday in the Open*, John Murray: London.

Ruskin, John (1893 [1864]) *Sesame and Lilies*, George Allen: London.

Sansom, Ian (2006) *The Mobile Library: Mr Dixon Disappears*, Harper Perennial: London. Reprinted with permission.

Sansom, I. (2005) *The Mobile Library: The Case of the Missing Books,* Harper Perennial: London. Reprinted with permission.

Savage, Sam (2009 [2008]) *Fermin*, Pheonix: London.

Scott, Walter (n.d. [1816]) *The Antiquary*, Collins: London.

Scott, Walter (n.d. [1815]) *Guy Mannering*, T. Nelson and Sons Ltd: London.

Scott, Walter, *Journal* see Anderson, W. E. K.

Sheffield, Lord (ed.) (1972 [1796]) *The Autobiography of Edward Gibbon*, Oxford University Press: Oxford.

Sheridan, Richard Brinsley (1988 [1773]) *The School for Scandal and Other Plays*, Harmondsworth: Penguin.

Sinclair, Iain (1995 [1987]) *White Chappell, Scarlet Tracings*, Vintage: London.

Škvorecký, Josef, 'The pleasures of the freedom to read' [1987] in D. Halpern (1990) (ed.) (*Antaeus: Literature as Pleasure*, Collins Harvill: London.

Smart, Elizabeth, for *Journals* see Wart, A. van.

Smith, Alexander (n.d. [1863]) 'Dreamthorpe' in *Dreamthorpe: A Book of Essays Written in the Country*, George Routledge and Sons Ltd: London.

Smith, Betty (1999 [1943]) *A Tree Grows in Brooklyn*, Reader's Digest Ltd: London.

Southey, Robert, for *Letters* see Currey, K.

Squire, J. C. (1927) 'On destroying books' in *Life at the Mermaid and Other Essays*, Kingsway Classics: London.

Sterne, Laurence (1986 [1768]) *A Sentimental Journey through France and Italy*, Penguin: London.

Stevenson, Robert Louis (1950 [1882]) 'A gossip on romance' in Elwin, M. (ed.) *The Essays of Robert Louis Stevenson*, Macdonald: London.

Stidger, W.L. (1922) *The Place of Books in the Life We Live*, George H. Duran and Co.: New York.

Swinnerton, F. (ed.) *The Journals of Arnold Bennett*, Penguin: London.

Taylor, Elizabeth (1991 [1957]) *Angel*, Virago Modern Classics.

Taylor, Elizabeth (2006 [1947]) *A View of the Harbour*, Virago Press: London.

Taylor, George, diary entries in S. Garfield (2004) *Our Hidden Lives*, The Ebury Press: London.

Thackeray, William Makepeace (1869) 'On a lazy, idle boy' and 'On some late great victories,' in *Roundabout Papers*, Smith, Elder and Co.: London.

Thackeray, William Makepeace (1987 [1848]) *Vanity Fair*, Harmondsworth: Penguin.

Thomas, Edward (1983 [1913]) *The Happy-go-Lucky Morgans*, Boydell Press: Woodbridge.

Thomas, Scarlett (2008 [2006]) *The End of Mr Y*, Canongate: Edinburgh. Reprinted with permission.

Thurber, James [1953] 'My own ten rules for a happy marriage' in A. Goodfellow (ed.) (2002) *Better to have Loafed and Lost: The Best of James Thurber*, Ebury Press: London.

Tolstoy, Leo trans. R. Edmunds (1978 [1876]) *Anna Karenin*, Harmondsworth: Penguin.

Torrington, John (1993 [1992]) *Swing Hammer Swing*, London: Secker and Warburg.

Trevelyan, G.O. (1893) *The Life and Letters of Lord Macaulay*, Longmans, Green and Co.: London.

Trollope, Anthony (1944 [1878]) *Is He Popenjoy?*, Oxford University Press: London.

Turgenev, Ivan trans. R. Edmunds (1975 [1861]) *Fathers and Sons*, Penguin: London.

Uzanne, Octave (1893) *The Book-Hunter in Paris: Studies Among the Bookstalls and the Quays*, Elliot Stock: London.

Walpole, H. (1926) *These Diversions: Reading,* Jarrolds: London.

Walsh, John (2008) 'When the literati come to party, it's time to clean up your bookshelves', *Independent,* 2nd December. Reprinted with permission.

Wart, A. van (ed.) (1992) *Necessary Secrets: The First Volume of Elizabeth Smart's Journals,* Paladin: London..

Welty, Eudora (1998) 'Listening' and 'A sweet devouring' in *Stories, Essays and Memoir,* Literary Classics of the United States: New York. 'Listening' reprinted by permission from ONE WRITER'S BEGINNING by Eudora Welty, 7–8, Cambridge, Mass.: Harvard University Press, Copyright © 1983, 1984 by Eudora Welty. 'A sweet devouring' reprinted by the permission of Russell and Volkening as agents for the author. Copyright © by Eudora Welty.

Wheeler, Harriet and Gavurin, David (1996) 'Here's where the story ends', *Reading, Writing and Arithmatic,* Parlaphone.

Whitlock, R. (1654) *Zoomatia,* in A.K. Croston (1949) *Two Seventeenth-Century Prefaces,* University Press of Liverpool: London.

Wilde, O. (1994) 'The decay of lying' [1891] in *The Complete Works,* HarperCollins: London.

Wilde, O. (1886) letter to *Pall Mall Gazette,* quoted in J. Gross (ed.) (1998) *New Oxford Book of English Prose,* Oxford University Press: London.

Wodehouse, P.G. (1987 [1958]) *Cocktail Time,* London: Penguin.

Wolfe, Thomas. (1984) [1935]) *Of Time and the River,* Penguin: Harmondsworth. Reprinted with the permission of Scribner, a division of Simon & Schuster, Inc., Copyright © 1963 by Fred Gitlin, Administrator, C.T.A. All rights reserved.

Woolf, L. (1945) 'Memoirs of an elderly man', in R. Lehman, E. Muir, D. Kilham Roberts and C. Day Lewis (eds) *Orion: A Miscellany,* Nicholson and Watson: London. Reprinted with permission of The University of Sussex and Society of Authors as the literary representative of Leonard Woolf.

Woolf, V., for *Diary* see Bell A. O.

Woolf, V. (2003 [1921]) 'A society' in *Monday or Tuesday,* Hesperus: London. Printed with permission of the Society of Authors as the literary representative of the Estate of Virginia Woolf.

Wright, Richard (1945 [1937]) *Black Boy: A Record of Childhood and Youth,* Victor Gollancz Ltd: London.

Wright, W.A. (ed.) (1901) *More Letters of Edward Fitzgerald,* Macmillan and Co.: London.

Zetland, Marquis of (1929) *The Letters of Disraeli to Lady Bradford and Lady Chesterfield, vol II,* Ernest Benn Limited: London.